PFS
First Choice
Applications
Made Easy

Paul Dlug

Assistant Professor
School of Business
Business Computer Information Systems
Hofsta University

Published by **Windcrest Books**
FIRST EDITION/FOURTH PRINTING

Library of Congress Cataloging-in-Publication Data

Dlug, Paul.
    PFS, First choice—applications made easy / by Paul Dlug.
        p.   cm.
    Includes index.
    ISBN 0-8306-2913-0 (pbk.)
    1. PFS, First choice (Computer program) I. Title.
QA76.754.D57   1987
005.36′9—dc19   87-19407
                                                                      CIP

TAB BOOKS Inc. offers software for sale. For information and a catalog, please contact TAB Software Department, Blue Ridge Summit, PA 17294-0850.

Questions regarding the content of this book should be addressed to:
Windcrest Books
Division of TAB BOOKS Inc.
Blue Ridge Summit, PA 17294-0850

Ron Powers: Director of Acquisitions
Marianne Krcma: Technical Editor
Katherine Brown: Production
Jaclyn B. Saunders: Series Design
Doug Robson: Cover Design

To my wife, Rita Marie, and our children, Paul, Laura, and Debra

Contents

Introduction

This book is a tutorial manual consisting of a series of business and home applications based on the PFS: First Choice Version 1.0 software program published by Software Publishing Corporation. Business application problems are solved using First Choice's powerful command structure.

You can take full advantage of the program's powerful features without any special training or prior computer knowledge because this book is designed to be a tutorial and not a reference guide. However, it could easily be used as a reference guide by using the appendices, glossary, and index at the back of the book.

This book covers the four major parts of the First Choice integrated program: word processing, file management, spreadsheet analysis, and electronic communications. It is strongly recommended that you follow the chapters in sequence because the commands are arranged in the order of difficulty and use.

This book is useful to the complete novice or the experienced programmer who needs to solve a particular problem because it emphasizes the "hands-on" approach or "learn by doing." Each problem starts with a business application where the commands are used to solve that particular problem. Each chapter has a series of figures to show you what the screen should look like as you proceed through the chapter.

The word processing chapters of this book enable you to create and edit documents, store and retrieve them, and print them out in a variety of styles. Once the document is created, you can refine and rephrase it to suit your needs.

You can compose the document at the keyboard and save it on a diskette to be revised or printed at a later date.

The management and report sections enable you to design a file, add and update data, and print it out in any format that you desire. A file holds information that is related to a specific type of application. For example, a file of customers would contain the names, addresses, and other information about a group of people who are customers of a particular firm.

The spreadsheet function enables you to create a row/column chart to do financial calculations such as budgeting and income statements. This row/column chart is called a spreadsheet. Electronic spreadsheets provide capabilities for generating and formatting worksheets in computer memory, and for entering and manipulating data within worksheets.

The communications function enables you to use First Choice to connect with information services or other computers. It can even dial the correct telephone number so that it can access this service.

Appendix A contains nine model business spreadsheet problems that are worked out with spreadsheet listing. This should give you ideas how this particular module can be used.

When you are finished with the tutorial part of this book, try creating your own word processing documents, files, and spreadsheets. Appendix B provides you with all the commands of First Choice organized by menu keys. This along with the help keys of the program should give you some added assistance.

PFS: First Choice can be used by homeowners, students, educators, business people, salespersons, engineers, or anyone who wants to learn how to use a simple but powerful software package for word processing, file management, spreadsheet analysis, and communications.

Chapter 1

Setting Up
PFS: First Choice

This chapter explains the nature of an integrated program, the hardware requirements of First Choice, how to install the program, and how to set up the program using both standard and nonstandard equipment.

WHAT IS AN INTEGRATED PROGRAM?

PFS: First Choice is an integrated software package that enables the user to perform word processing, file management, spreadsheet analysis, and data communications from within one software package. These different software applications can be created and used within the same program. If you use several different application programs, on the other hand, data created in one program can be accessed only by the program that is in use. To use the data in another application, the user must leave the program that he or she is currently operating and then must load the other program. This can cause some confusing disk-switching to go from one application to another.

Software integration enables the user to share and transfer data among different applications. For example, you can merge information from a data file to create a form letter in a word processing document. You can add the tabular presentation of spreadsheet figures to a word processing document to demonstrate market analysis.

The advantage of using an integrated software package is that the same commands that are used to insert text in a word processing document are used to insert text in a file or a spreadsheet. This set of common commands enables you to go swiftly from one application to another. Data that is entered in one application, such as a file, can be made available to another application, such as a personalized form letter. With First Choice you can "cut and paste" from one application to another.

BACKUPS

The PFS: First Choice program and diskettes are provided on both 5 ¼ inch disks and 3½ inch disks. It is always a good idea to make backups of all your disks. The first thing that you should do is make a backup of First Choice's program disk and dictionary disk. Use the DOS copy or diskcopy commands to back them up and place the originals in a safe place. In a similar manner, you should make a backup of the data disk that you will create for this book.

HARDWARE REQUIREMENTS

To use PFS: First Choice you must have an IBM or IBM-compatible computer with at least 256K of memory, a monochrome or color monitor, DOS 2.0 or later, one or two floppy disk drives, or one floppy disk drive and a hard disk, an optional printer, an optional modem, and an optional mouse. First Choice will also support the 8087 and 80287 coprocessors. The default printer at start-up time is a parallel printer. The default modem at start-up time is a Hayes-compatible modem and a touch-tone phone.

SETTING UP FIRST CHOICE

If you are using two floppy disk drives, follow these steps:

1. Boot up your computer system with DOS.
2. Remove DOS and insert the PFS: First Choice program disk in drive A and the Dictionary Disk in drive B.
3. At the A> DOS prompt, type First.
4. The Main Menu of First Choice now appears as shown in Fig. 1-1.

The Main Menu is used to choose your options, such as writing a letter or memo, creating a file, setting up a report, creating a spreadsheet, getting an existing file, communicating with another computer or database, setting up your equipment, or leaving First Choice by exiting to DOS.

USING A HARD DISK

Copy First Choice to any directory by typing **7 Set Up Equipment** from the Main Menu. While in the Set Up Menu shown in Fig 1-2, type **4 Install to a hard disk.**

Type c:\choice to install First Choice on drive C in directory \choice. When you are finished, press the Enter or Return key to copy all files to the hard disk. Type **5 Return to Main Menu** to continue on with First Choice or

```
                    PFS:First Choice
                       Main Menu

          1-Create a document
          2-Create a file folder
          3-Create a report
          4-Create a spreadsheet
          5-Get an existing file
          6-Connect to another computer
          7-Set up equipment
          8-Leave First Choice




    _____
          Copyright 1986 by Software Publishing Corporation
  ↑or↓ to choose a selection, and then press ←┘; Or press F1 for Help.
```

Fig. 1-1. PFS: First Choice Main Menu.

```
                       Set up Menu


           1-Select color or no color
           2-Select a printer
           3-Select a modem
           4-Install to a hard disk
           5-Return to Main Menu




  ↑or·↓to choose a selection, and then press ←┘; Or press F1 for Help.
```

Fig. 1-2. The Set Up Menu.

stay in the Set Up Menu if you have other changes to make as discussed in the next section. To run First Choice from the DOS prompt, type cd \ choice followed by typing First. You can type in all commands in uppercase and lowercase.

SETTING UP NONSTANDARD EQUIPMENT

If you have any nonstandard equipment that does not match the hardware requirements discussed in the section on hardware requirements, you will have to set up First Choice. This would include having a serial printer, a non-Hayes compatible modem, or a rotary dial telephone.

To access the Set Up Menu, type 7 Set Up Equipment from the Main Menu followed by pressing the Return key. This will give you the Set Up Menu that was shown in Fig. 1-2. Option 1, Select color or no color, enables you to choose different sets of colors for different color monitors and graphics cards, as shown in Fig. 1-3. If you have a monochrome monitor, select the black and white option. Use this even if you have a color graphics card installed in your computer. If you have a color monitor with a color graphics card, you may select from the two color palettes. If you are not sure which one to use, try each one and see which one is to your liking.

Option 2, Select a printer, enables you to select a printer from a list that is given with the program. The default value is a parallel printer. The default parallel printer port is called PRN: or LPT1:. Figure 1-4 shows a screen dump

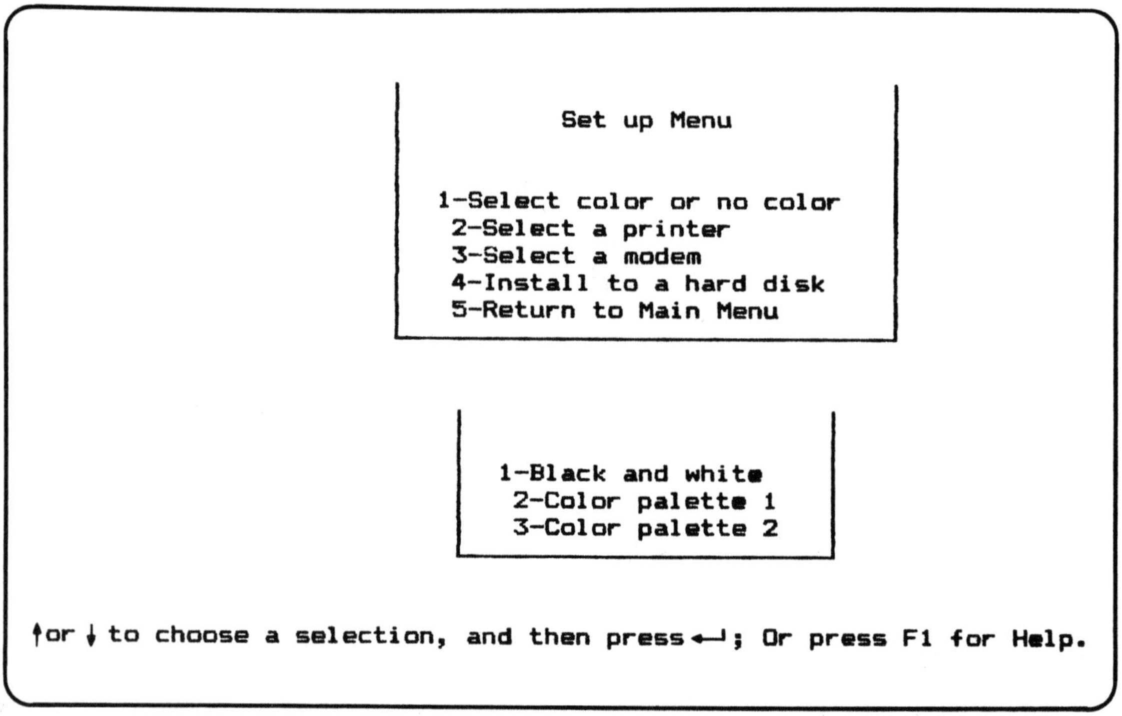

```
                        Set up Menu


              1-Select color or no color
               2-Select a printer
               3-Select a modem
               4-Install to a hard disk
               5-Return to Main Menu



               1-Black and white
               2-Color palette 1
               3-Color palette 2


↑or ↓ to choose a selection, and then press ←⏎; Or press F1 for Help.
```

Fig. 1-3. The Set Up Menu for color or monochrome screens.

```
Choose printer: 13
Printer connects to (PRN,COM1,COM2,LPT1,LPT2,LPT3): PRINTER

  11. Epson EX-800          16. Epson LQ-1500
  12. Epson FX-80/100 III   17. Epson MX-80/100 III
  13. Epson FX-85/185/286   18. Epson RX-80/100
  14. Epson LX-80           19. HP LJet COUR Land
  15. Epson LQ-800/1000     20. HP LJet COUR Port

Esc to cancel        PgUp, PgDn -- more        ↵ to continue
```

Fig. 1-4. The Set Up Menu for printers.

of 10 possible printers that you could use. By using the PgUp and PgDn keys, you can see many more of them. All the most popular and common printers are listed. Check your printer manual to see the type of printer you have and to see if it is serial or parallel. If your printer is unlisted, press 1, the unlisted printer option. After you are finished naming your printer, press the Tab key to advance the cursor to **Printer connects to**. It is here that you tell the printer if it is serial (COM1 or COM2) or parallel (LPT1, LPT2, LPT3, or PRN). The default setting is parallel, so there is no need to do anything if your printer is parallel but press the Return key. If your printer is serial, you will be asked the printer settings that can be obtained from your printer manual. After you are finished typing in the various printer settings, press the Return key to save them.

```
Modem: 12
Modem connects to (COM1,COM2): COM1
Telephone line is rotary or touch-tone (R/T): T

  1.  Unlisted modem           6.  Anchor Lightning 24
  2.  Acoustic                 7.  Bizcmp PC:Intl1Mdm EXT
  3.  Anchor Signalman Mk XII  8.  Bizcmp PC:Intl1Mdm XT
  4.  Anchor Volksmodem 12     9.  Hayes Smartmodem 300
  5.  Anchor Express          10.  Hayes Smartmodem 1200/B

Esc to cancel        PgDn -- more        ↵ to continue
```

Fig. 1-5. The Set Up Menu for modems.

Choosing option 3, **Select a modem,** followed by pressing the Return key enables you to select a modem from a list of modems. The default is a Hayes-compatible modem. Figure 1-5 shows you a list of the first 10 modems that are listed. Again, just as in printers, the most common and popular are listed. After you select the modem, press the Tab key and you will be asked **Modem connects to.** The two options that are listed COM1 and COM2 are for serial ports. After checking your modem manual, type in the name of the port. First Choice also asks if you are using a rotary or touch-tone telephone. The default setting is touch-tone. Type **R** if you are using a rotary telephone, followed by pressing the Return key. This will save the information that you have typed in.

After you have finished making changes to the Set Up Menu, press 5, **Return to Main Menu,** to save changes and exit to the main menu.

USING A MOUSE

First Choice enables you to use a mouse to move the cursor, obtain a menu, select a menu item, exit a menu, and choose text. You must use either a Microsoft or Mouse Systems mouse which must be set up each time before running First Choice.

Chapter 2

Resume:

Creating a Document

In this chapter, you learn how to create and edit a document. In the edit mode this involves inserting and deleting characters, words, lines, and paragraphs, and copying and moving lines and paragraphs. You also learn how to use the various print styles, the spelling checker, and the find and replace functions of First Choice. You will be able to create your own document, save it to disk, and, finally, load it from disk.

BACKGROUND

Word processing can be thought of as typing with a computer. The way text is entered with a computer to obtain the finished product is nearly the same as with a typewriter, but you will find the job easier with a computer. Essentially, the computer becomes a typewriter that is capable of doing many more operations. The words of your document go into the computer's memory rather than onto paper, so you can easily correct and adjust your text. Keying errors may be corrected; words, sentences, paragraphs, or pages may be added or deleted; margins can be set; page lengths can be defined; and many other functions that involve the manipulation of the written word can be performed. Word processing makes it easy to produce quality printed output. The word processing module of First Choice lets you create printing effects, justify margins, center text, and much more.

Word processing is not just typing and printing. You can use it to compose a customized letter made up of standardized paragraphs. Each of these standardized paragraphs is stored separately in the computer's memory. You can insert data into form letters and generate mailing labels or envelopes. You can store copies of text and then have them ready for instant retrieval and printing months later.

The person who benefits the most from word processing is the writer. Business people can save time by writing their own letters on a word processor. There is no need to dictate the letter, wait for someone else to type it, and then proofread it. All adjustments and improvements can be made immediately.

CREATING YOUR OWN DOCUMENT

To create your own document, go to the main menu and press 1, the **Create a document** key. If the line is shaded, you can select it by pressing the Return key. The document you type until you save it (by giving it a name) is called the *Working Copy*. If you accidentally get out of the document entry, you can always retrieve the Working Copy by going to the main menu and pressing 5, **Getting an existing file.** Type **Working Copy** as the name of the file that you wish to retrieve. When you press 1, the **Create a document** key, Fig. 2-1 appears.

To enter any of the major options of First Choice, you go into the Main Menu. If at any time you get lost and want to return to the Main Menu, press the ESC key. The ESC key will always let you exit the current program and return to the Main Menu. It will also remind you to save any document so that it won't get lost. The top line of Fig. 2-1 shows the function keys that you can

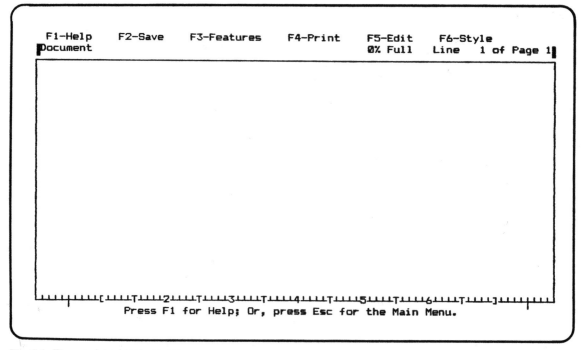

Fig. 2-1. The word processor screen.

press to obtain other menus. All the function keys are located on the left side of the keyboard or along the top of the keyboard above the number keys. This depends on the brand and model of the computer that you are using. First Choice uses the first six function keys (F1 through F6). You will be using some of the function keys as you start creating your own document.

The next line (second from the top of the screen) tells you the name of the document on which you are working. If there is no name on the screen, it assumes that you are in the Working Copy, as you now are. Toward the right side of the line, it tells you how much of the computer's memory you are using. As you start typing in the document, you will notice the number increase from 0% toward the 100% figure. As your document approaches 100%, you will save what you are doing and create a new document. Several documents may be connected or joined together when they are printed. Document size is never a problem unless you are writing exceedingly long letters or are writing a book.

The last item on the second line shows the position of the cursor (the blinking underline). As you move the cursor, you will notice that the line number will change. Cursor movement will be discussed in the next section. When you create a new document, the cursor is always at Line 1 of Page 1. The cursor indicates the point at which the next character will be entered.

At the bottom of the screen is a line that resembles a ruler. The letter T on the ruler indicates the present positions of the tab settings. In Chapter 3, you will learn how to insert and delete your own tab settings. The cursor position is indicated on the ruler. As you move the cursor, the movement will be shown on the bottom of the screen. You can then tell the column number the cursor is on by reading the markings on the ruler. Remember the line and page numbers are on the second line of the screen, while the column of the line you are on is indicated on the ruler at the bottom of the screen.

CURSOR KEYS

On the right side of the keyboard are the four arrow, or *cursor*, keys. Try moving them around to get a feel for how they work. The right and left arrows are used to move the cursor one character to the right and one character to the left, respectively. The up and down arrows move the cursor up or down one line.

The Backspace key moves and erases the character to the left of the cursor. The PgUp and PgDn keys will help you get to the parts of the document that you cannot see on the screen by moving up or down one screen at a time. If you press the Home key, you will arrive at the beginning of the line, while the End key moves the cursor to the end of the line. By pressing simultaneously the CTRL and Home keys you will arrive at the beginning of the document. By pressing simultaneously the CTRL and End keys you will arrive at the end of the document.

The Tab and Backtab keys move the cursor to the right and left. All tabs except the first are 10 characters. The first tab moves the cursor five columns from the left margin. Notice that as you move the cursor, the column position on the ruler changes and the line number changes.

ENTERING TEXT

You are now ready to enter text into the Working Copy. Figure 2-2 shows the beginning part of a resume that you will type.

Notice that this document has a name: **RESUME.DOC.** Ignore this right now. In the next section you will learn how to save the document that you are working on. This document also takes up 1% of the computer's memory, as you can see on the second line from the top of the screen. The full document is shown in Fig. 2-3. Type it in.

Notice that there are some typing errors in the resume. Leave them in, together with any other ones you accidentally type; you will fix them later. You will also notice that as you type in the resume, the top part scrolls off the screen. If the resume or any other document is long, it will be impossible to see the whole document on the screen.

When you are finished typing in the document, you can use the PgUp or PgDn keys to move the cursor up and down the document one screen length at a time. You can also use the CTRL Home key to move the cursor to the beginning of the document, and the CTRL End to move the cursor to the end of the document. Try experimenting with all the cursor movements that were mentioned in the last section.

Most of the beginning lines of the resume involve pressing the Return key to advance to the next line. If the line is too long, as in the end of the resume, the program will *word wrap* to the next line. This will be done automatically by the program. Word wrap means that additional words at the end of the

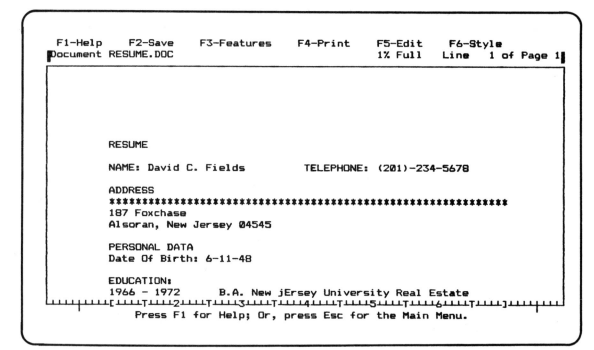

Fig. 2-2. The beginning of the resume screen.

```
RESUME

NAME: David C. Fields          TELEPHONE: (201)-234-5678

ADDRESS
**********************************************************************
187 Foxchase
Alsoran, New Jersey 04545

PERSONAL DATA
Date Of Birth: 6-11-48

EDUCATION:
1966 - 1972        B.A. New jErsey University Real Estate

1962 - 1966        High School Academic Diploma
                   Blue Jay High School
EXPERIENCE:
1980 - Present     Real Real Estate Broker
                   Take-A-Home Realty
                   Strawberry Foelds, New Jersey

1974 - 1980        Credit Manager
                   Red Star Oil Company Cutty Shark, New York

MILITARY SERVICE:
1972 - 1974        U.S. AArmy - Corporal; Quartermaster Corp;
Taught business clases to to servicemen during term of
service; Served one year in Spain as a Spanish interpreter;
Received Army Commendation Ribbon

LICENSE:
1972 - New Jersey Brokers License

AWARDS:
Outstanding Take-A-Home Real Estate Broker for 1985;
Awarded to the broker who is both civic minded and has the
most sales.
```

Fig. 2-3. The complete resume.

sentence will automatically be added to the beginning of the next line. There is no need to press the Return key unless you want to advance to a new paragraph.

EDITING THE DOCUMENT

There are basically two functions that you can perform on a document: inserting and deleting letters, words, lines, and paragraphs. When you begin to use First Choice you are in the Replacement mode. Notice that the cursor is represented by an underline. When you are in this mode, you can just type over any letters or words that you wish to erase. If you press the Del key, the word under the cursor is deleted and the other letters are joined together to fill in the missing space. If you press the Backspace key, the letter to the left of the cursor is erased and, again, the other letters are joined together to fill in the gap.

If you press the Ins key, you go into the Insert mode. Notice that the cursor takes the shape of a small rectangle. Whatever letters you type will be inserted at the position of the cursor. You can switch from the Insert mode to the Replacement mode by pressing the Ins key.

Looking at the resume, you see that the word Army has two A's. You would like to delete one of them. Move the cursor to line 27, column 33 by using the cursor keys, and press the Del key. This will erase one of the A's from the screen. You can always tell the line number you are on by looking at the top right of the screen. It tells the line number and the page number of the document. At the bottom of the screen, the ruler enables you to count off the column numbers.

On line 28 column 27, notice that the word "classes" is misspelled. There is only one letter s instead of two. If you are not in the Insert mode, go there by pressing the Ins key. Go to line 28, column 27 and type in the letter s. Notice how the letter is inserted into the word and all the other letters are adjusted around it.

You would like to insert the word "Drive" in line 7, column 23. Place the cursor in that position and just type in the word.

On line 19, column 27, you would like to eliminate the word "Real" because you see there are two of them. There are several ways you could do this. One way is to place the cursor on the letter R and press the Del key four times. A second way is to place the cursor in the space to the right of the letter d and press the Backspace key four times. The third and most efficient way is to use the speed key, Alt-W, as shown in the Find It Quick chart. Place the cursor on the R and simultaneously press the Alt key and the W key. This will eliminate the word in only one operation regardless of the length of the word.

SAVING A DOCUMENT

You can save a file at any time by pressing the F2 (Save) key followed by pressing the 1 key, Save a copy of this document. First Choice will prompt you for the name of the file. The name of a file can be up to eight characters in length. It can start with any letter, number, or special character. Some possible names are Resume, #1Letter, R2D2 and @HOME.

If you are using a two floppy-disk system, place a blank formatted disk in drive B: after removing the Dictionary Disk. Type B:.

Type in the name RESUME (or any other document name that you wish) followed by pressing the Return key. The name of the document should represent what is in the document itself. For example, you could have named this document A or any other combination of letters or numbers. These would be easily forgotten at a later date.

There is no need to type in the extension .DOC. If a file already exists with the same file name, First Choice asks if you wish to replace it. Don't forget to use the drive name if you are saving the document on a particular drive. It is always a good idea to periodically save your file as you progress through a document so you don't lose it in a possible power loss.

First Choice can also save programs as ASCII files if you add the extension .ASC instead of .DOC to the document name. ASCII files are used in many word processing programs and these files can be exchanged with them. Text styles, margins, headers, and footers are not saved with an ASCII file.

THE HELP KEY

If at any time you don't know what to do or what keys to press, press the F1 (Help) key. The Help key saves a lot of time by eliminating the need to look for information in the manual.

Figure 2-4 shows a Help screen for the document you just retrieved. There are many Help screens that are available to you at any time if you forget a command or don't want to look in the First Choice manual. You may leave the Help screen by pressing the ESC key.

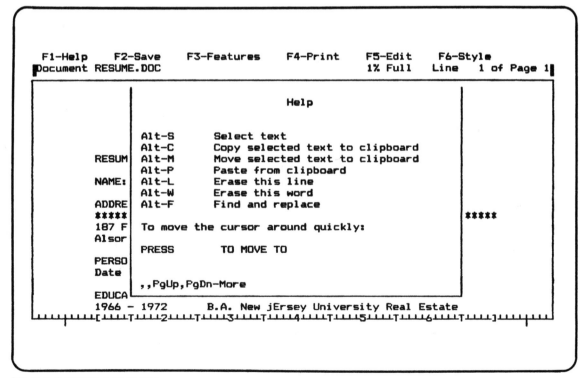

Fig. 2-4. A sample help screen.

CENTERING A LINE AND USING BOLDFACE PRINT

Looking at your resume you decide that you want the word RESUME in the first line to be both centered and have boldface print. Place the cursor anywhere on line 1 and press the F6 (Style) function key. Figure 2-5 appears.

It contains a box that has all the style formats. Notice the dot next to **7 Single Space.** This shows that the line is already single-spaced. To center the line, press 9, **Center.** The word RESUME is immediately centered on the line. To have the word printed in boldface, you must tell First Choice that you wish to use the boldface style on the whole word. Press the F5 (Edit) key and the edit box will appear on the right side of the screen, as shown in Fig. 2-6. Notice that you could have also erased the word ''Real'' discussed in the previous section by pressing the F5 Edit key following by pressing the 8 key, **Erase this word.**

Place the cursor on the letter R of RESUME. Press 1, **Select text.** Highlight the word RESUME by using the cursor keys. Now press the F6 (Style) key again and press the 1 key, **Boldface.** The word is highlighted on the screen compared to the other surrounding words. The word will be printed on the paper in boldface type only if your printer possesses this capability. If you don't select the whole word, only the first letter of the word will be printed in boldface.

Look at the other styles in the style box. As you start typing your own document or using the resume document, try experimenting with the other types such as underline, italics, superscript, subscript, and erase. Remember that these depend on your printer. You can change from single- to double-spacing within

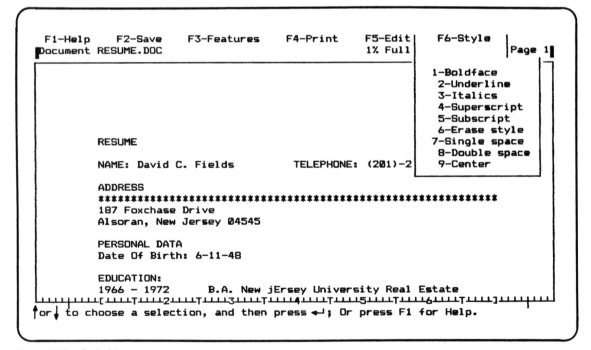

Fig. 2-5. The Style Menu.

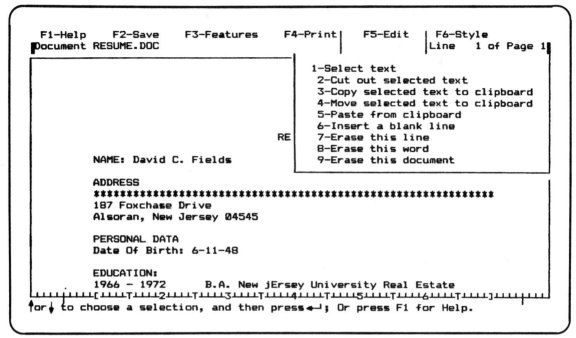

Fig. 2-6. The Edit Menu.

a document by pressing 8, **Double space**. First Choice will keep on double-spacing from the line at which the cursor is on until it encounters a single-space command.

COPYING TEXT

Notice that the row of asterisks in column 6 seems to enhance the resume. You would like to copy that row and insert it below the other headings such as Personal Data, Education, etc.

You must first select the text to be copied. Move the cursor to line 6, column 1 and press the F5 (Edit) key. Remember from the last section that you select text before you change its type style, copy it, or move it. Press 1, **Select text**. Highlight the whole line of asterisks by moving the cursor to the end of the line by pressing the End key. Now press F5 **Edit** followed by pressing 3, **Copy selected text to clipboard**. The *clipboard* is a holding area where a copy of the text is placed. The original text is still in the document.

Notice that the highlight on the line is missing. Move the cursor to line 11, column 1 and press the F5 key, **Edit**. Press 5, **Paste from clipboard**. This will automatically insert the line of asterisks in line 11 after the Personal Data. Notice that the original row of asterisks is still in line 6 and, if you could see it, there is a row of asterisks in the clipboard.

In a similar manner, place the cursor on line 15, column 1 and press the F5 (Edit) key. Press 5 (Paste from clipboard) to insert the row of asterisks after the Education heading. Place the cursor on line 21, column 1 and press the F5

(Edit) key. Press 5, **Paste from clipboard,** to insert the row of asterisks after the Experience heading. Place the cursor on line 30, column 1 and press the F5 key. Press 5 (Paste from clipboard) to insert the row of asterisks after the Military Service heading. Place the cursor on line 37, column 1 and press the F5 key, then press 5 to insert the row of asterisks after the License heading.

Repeat this process at line 41, column 1 to insert the final row of asterisks after the Awards heading. The final document should look like Fig. 2-7.

PRINTING THE DOCUMENT

Assuming you have a printer, you would like to print out the complete document as shown in Fig. 2-7. You must make sure that your printer is connected to the computer and turned on. Press the F4 key, **Print,** and the Print menu is displayed as shown in Fig. 2-8.

Because you want to print the whole document, press the 1 **Print this document** key. When you do this, another menu is displayed as shown in Fig. 2-9.

The Print Options menu lets you print any range of pages you want if you have a document several pages long. You can print several copies of any document by typing in the number of copies you want. You can also print a correspondence copy and/or compressed type copy if your printer has these capabilities. This menu lets you justify a document so the left and right sides have the same margins. It lets you pause between pages to insert single sheets of paper if you are using business stationery. It enables you to print to the printer (the default value), to screen, or to a disk file. It also allows you to change the left margin by indenting it to whatever you would like.

To change any of these factors, use the Tab key to move over to the factor you want to change and type in the new value. Press the Return or Enter key to exit the Print Options menu.

First Choice will now ask you to put a new page in the printer and press the Return or Enter key. The document will now be printed and will look like the one that was shown in Fig. 2-7.

COPYING TO A NEW DOCUMENT

A document can be copied to a new document in its entirety by saving it under a new name. This is useful if there are a lot of changes being made and you want to see a record of the changes. For example, going from RESUME.DOC to RESUME1.DOC shows a record of all the changes up to that point.

You can also save part of a document to a new document. In this example, you would like to save the name and address of the resume to a separate file because you use it a lot. Move the cursor to line 3, column 1. Press the F5 (Edit) key followed by pressing 1, **Select text.** You must first select the text that you wish to copy to a new document. Press Return six times to highlight the text that you wish to have copied. Press the F2 (Save) key. Because you want to save only a portion of the text, press 2, **Selected text only.** First Choice

```
                         RESUME

NAME: David C. Fields          TELEPHONE: (201)-234-5678

ADDRESS
*****************************************************************
187 Foxchase Drive
Alsoran, New Jersey 04545

PERSONAL DATA
*****************************************************************
Date Of Birth: 6-11-48

EDUCATION:
*****************************************************************
1966 - 1972          B.A. New jErsey University Real Estate

1962 - 1966          High School Academic Diploma
                     Blue Jay High School
EXPERIENCE:
*****************************************************************
1980 - Present       Real Estate Broker
                     Take-A-Home Realty
                     Strawberry Foelds, New Jersey

1974 - 1980          Credit Manager
                     Red Star Oil Company Cutty Shark, New York

MILITARY SERVICE:
*****************************************************************
1972 - 1974          U.S. Army - Corporal; Quartermaster Corp;
Taught business classes to to servicemen during term of
service; Served one year in Spain as a Spanish interpreter;
Received Army Commendation Ribbon

LICENSE:
*****************************************************************
1972 - New Jersey Brokers License

AWARDS:
*****************************************************************
Outstanding Take-A-Home Real Estate Broker for 1985;
Awarded to the broker who is both civic minded and has the
most sales.
```

Fig. 2-7. A resume that demonstrates the Copy statement.

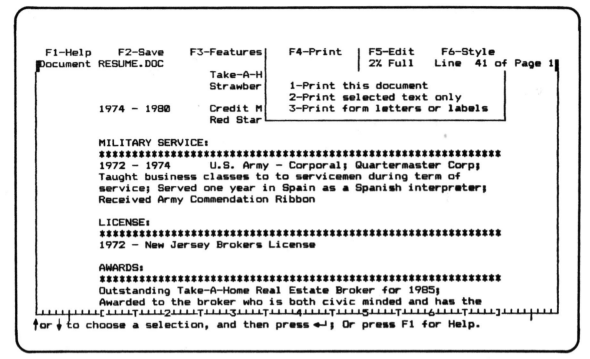

```
 F1-Help    F2-Save    F3-Features|  F4-Print  | F5-Edit    F6-Style
Document RESUME.DOC                |           | 2% Full   Line  41 of Page 1
                        Take-A-H   | 1-Print this document
                        Strawber   | 2-Print selected text only
           1974 - 1980  Credit M   | 3-Print form letters or labels
                        Red Star

           MILITARY SERVICE:
           ************************************************************
           1972 - 1974     U.S. Army - Corporal; Quartermaster Corp;
           Taught business classes to to servicemen during term of
           service; Served one year in Spain as a Spanish interpreter;
           Received Army Commendation Ribbon

           LICENSE:
           ************************************************************
           1972 - New Jersey Brokers License

           AWARDS:
           ************************************************************
           Outstanding Take-A-Home Real Estate Broker for 1985;
           Awarded to the broker who is both civic minded and has the
|...........[....T....2....T....3....T....4....T....5....T....6....T....]........|
↑or ↓ to choose a selection, and then press ↵; Or press F1 for Help.
```

Fig. 2-8. The Print Menu.

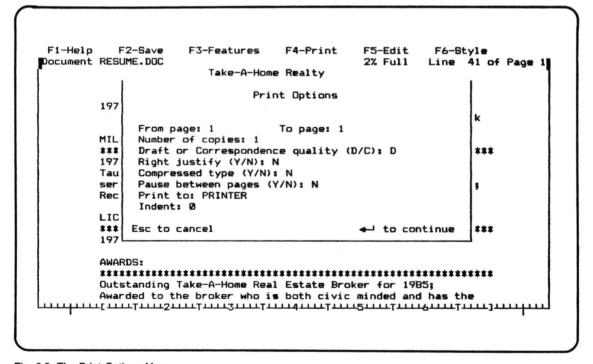

```
 F1-Help    F2-Save    F3-Features    F4-Print    F5-Edit    F6-Style
Document RESUME.DOC                                2% Full   Line  41 of Page 1
                        Take-A-Home Realty
                              Print Options
           197
                                                               k
                   From page: 1         To page: 1
           MIL     Number of copies: 1
           ***     Draft or Correspondence quality (D/C): D       ***
           197     Right justify (Y/N): N
           Tau     Compressed type (Y/N): N
           ser     Pause between pages (Y/N): N                   ;
           Rec     Print to: PRINTER
                   Indent: 0
           LIC
           ***  Esc to cancel                ↵ to continue        ***
           197

           AWARDS:
           ************************************************************
           Outstanding Take-A-Home Real Estate Broker for 1985;
           Awarded to the broker who is both civic minded and has the
|...........[....T....2....T....3....T....4....T....5....T....6....T....]........|
```

Fig. 2-9. The Print Options Menu.

now asks you for the name that you wish for the file. Type **NAME_ADD**. That file name, which contains the name and address, will now be saved on the disk.

MOVING WITHIN A DOCUMENT

Looking at your sample resume, you would like to move the section Military Service to the end. You must first select the text before you can use it. Move the cursor to line 29, column 1. Press the F5 (Edit) key. Press 1, **Select text,** followed by pressing the Return key seven times. This will highlight the text that you wish to move. Press the F5 key again and press 4, **Move selected text to clipboard.**

Move the cursor to line 39, column 1 and press the F5 key. Press 5, **Paste from Clipboard,** to move the text into that line. The new resume should appear as Fig. 2-10.

DELETING TEXT

Looking at the resume, you see that the section Personal Data is discriminatory and should be removed. Place the cursor on line 10, column 1 and press the F5 key to edit. Press 1, **Select text,** and press the Return key four times to include the blank line after the date of birth. Press the F5 key followed by pressing 2, **Cut out selected text.** That section is now removed as shown in Fig. 2-11.

You could also have deleted that section by erasing the four lines, but this would take more steps. If you change your mind and decide that you didn't want it erased, you can press 5, **Paste from clipboard,** or use the ALT-P speed key. Remember that the clipboard will always retain the last item that you erased.

INSERTING ONE DOCUMENT INTO ANOTHER

It is also possible to insert one document into another document. Figure 2-12 shows a document called Outside Interests that you wish inserted into the resume. You must first save the document that you are working on by pressing the F2 (Save) key followed by pressing 1, **Save a copy of this document.** When the program asks for a name to save it under, type RESUME or any other name that you wish to use.

You must now create another document as shown in Fig. 2-12. Before you create another document, you must erase the Working Copy of the document. If you called the document RESUME, the document is now saved under two names on your disk: RESUME and Working Copy.

Type in the paragraph shown in Fig. 2-12. If you make a mistake, use the editing techniques discussed earlier to fix it. When you are finished, save it by pressing the F2 (Save) key followed by pressing 1, **Save a copy of this document.** When the program prompts you for a name, call it OUTSIDEI for outside interest, or any other name that you wish. You will now have two documents on your disk: RESUME and OUTSIDEI.

You must now retrieve the document called RESUME. Return to the Main Menu by pressing the ESC key. Press 5, **Getting an existing file.** When it asks for the name of the file, type RESUME.

```
                            RESUME

NAME: David C. Fields            TELEPHONE: (201)-234-5678

ADDRESS
***************************************************************
187 Foxchase Drive
Alsoran, New Jersey 04545

PERSONAL DATA
***************************************************************
Date Of Birth: 6-11-48

EDUCATION:
***************************************************************
1966 - 1972        B.A. New jErsey University Real Estate

1962 - 1966        High School Academic Diploma
                   Blue Jay High School
EXPERIENCE:
***************************************************************
1980 - Present     Real Estate Broker
                   Take-A-Home Realty
                   Strawberry Foelds, New Jersey

1974 - 1980        Credit Manager
                   Red Star Oil Company Cutty Shark, New York

LICENSE:
***************************************************************
1972 - New Jersey Brokers License

AWARDS:
***************************************************************
Outstanding Take-A-Home Real Estate Broker for 1985;
Awarded to the broker who is both civic minded and has the
most sales.

MILITARY SERVICE:
***************************************************************
1972 - 1974        U.S. Army - Corporal; Quartermaster Corp;
Taught business classes to to servicemen during term of
service; Served one year in Spain as a Spanish interpreter;
Received Army Commendation Ribbon
```

Fig. 2-10. A resume that demonstrates the Move statement.

```
                              RESUME
NAME: David C. Fields         TELEPHONE: (201)-234-5678

ADDRESS
********************************************************
187 Foxchase Drive
Alsoran, New Jersey 04545

EDUCATION:
********************************************************
1966 - 1972        B.A. New jErsey University Real Estate

1962 - 1966        High School Academic Diploma
                   Blue Jay High School

EXPERIENCE:
********************************************************
1980 - Present     Real Estate Broker
                   Take-A-Home Realty
                   Strawberry Foelds, New Jersey

1974 - 1980        Credit Manager
                   Red Star Oil Company Cutty Shark, New York

LICENSE:
********************************************************
1972 - New Jersey Brokers License

AWARDS:
********************************************************
Outstanding Take-A-Home Real Estate Broker for 1985;
Awarded to the broker who is both civic minded and has the
most sales.

MILITARY SERVICE:
********************************************************
1972 - 1974      U.S. Army - Corporal; Quartermaster Corp;
Taught business classes to to servicemen during term of
service; Served one year in Spain as a Spanish interpreter;
Received Army Commendation Ribbon
```

Fig. 2-11. A resume that demonstrates the Cut Out statement.

Move the cursor to line 30, column 1 and press the F2 (Save) key. The Save menu is shown in Fig. 2-13.

Press 3, Merge another document. The program will now ask you:

Merge which file:

```
OUTSIDE INTERESTS:
************************************************************
Vice-President of the local Strawberry Fields Real Estate
Association; Captain of the Gappha Bowling Team; Member of
the Alsoran Beer Can Collecting Team; Lifetime member of
Friends-Of-Animals Association; Member of the Love-To-Garden
Club; Member of local Dentist Advisory Group
```

Fig. 2-12. An "outside interests" paragraph for the resume.

Type OUTSIDEI.DOC or use the cursor keys to highlight the files on the disk and press the Return or Enter key.

REMEMBER, if your data disk is in drive B type:

B:OUTSIDEI.DOC.

INSERTING A BLANK LINE

The merger worked on the screen, but it would be better if there was a blank line on line 37, column 1. Place the cursor on that line and column and press the F5 key. Press 6, Insert a blank line. A blank line is now inserted. A blank line can also be inserted by pressing the Return or Enter key while in the Insert mode. The blank line along with the merged files are shown in Fig. 2-14.

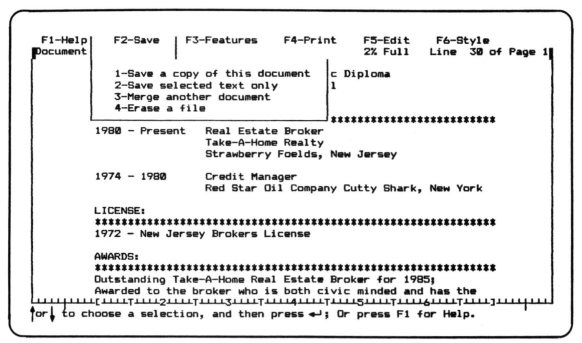

Fig. 2-13. The Save Menu.

```
                          RESUME
NAME: David C. Fields        TELEPHONE: (201)-234-5678

ADDRESS
*************************************************************
187 Foxchase Drive
Alsoran, New Jersey 04545

EDUCATION:
*************************************************************
1966 - 1972      B.A. New jErsey University Real Estate

1962 - 1966      High School Academic Diploma
                 Blue Jay High School

EXPERIENCE:
*************************************************************
1980 - Present   Real Estate Broker
                 Take-A-Home Realty
                 Strawberry Foelds, New Jersey

1974 - 1980      Credit Manager
                 Red Star Oil Company Cutty Shark, New York

LICENSE:
*************************************************************
1972 - New Jersey Brokers License

OUTSIDE INTERESTS:
*************************************************************
Vice-President of the local Strawberry Fields Real Estate
Association; Captain of the Gappha Bowling Team; Member of
the Alsoran Beer Can Collecting Team; Lifetime member of
Friends-Of-Animals Association; Member of the Love-To-Garden
Club; Member of local Dentist Advisory Group

AWARDS:
*************************************************************
Outstanding Take-A-Home Real Estate Broker for 1985;
Awarded to the broker who is both civic minded and has the
most sales.

MILITARY SERVICE:
*************************************************************
1972 - 1974      U.S. Army - Corporal; Quartermaster Corp;
Taught business classes to to servicemen during term of
service; Served one year in Spain as a Spanish interpreter;
Received Army Commendation Ribbon
```

Fig. 2-14. A resume with merged files.

DELETING A LINE

In a similar manner, you can also delete a line (blank or otherwise) by pressing the F5 key and pressing 7, **Erase this line.** You can also use the speed key, Alt-L, to accomplish the same task.

USING THE SPELLING CHECKER

First Choice can check the spelling of your document through the use of the spelling checker in the Features section of the menu. First Choice has a dictionary file of about 75,000 words. There is space for approximately 6,000 more words that you can add in a personal dictionary.

Each word in the file is compared to the master dictionary to see if it is contained there. When differences are found, disputed words are highlighted. The user of the program then decides if the highlighted words should be corrected or not. The spelling checker cannot distinguish between the correct use of words, such as typing ''large'' for ''lodge.'' Because both of these words are valid words, errors in usage are not detected.

The spelling checker allows the user to make entries in the personal dictionary. Users can add proper names, technical words, and unusual words that are used frequently. For example, if you do a lot of work in the medical profession, frequently used medical terms might be saved in the personal dictionary. This feature prevents situations in which names and special terms are marked repeatedly as misspelled.

You would like to check the spelling of the document from the beginning. Move the cursor to the beginning of the document by pressing the CTRL Home keys. This is necessary because the spelling checker starts at the word the cursor is on or the word to the right of the cursor. Because you want all the words in the document checked, you move the cursor to the beginning of the document.

Press the F3 (Features) key and then 2, **Check spelling.** Be sure the Dictionary Disk is in drive B if you are using a two floppy-disk system. If you have the wrong disk in the wrong drive, First Choice will prompt you to insert the correct disk. You will notice at the bottom right of the screen that each word of the document is flashed as it is checked. The first word that it stops at is ''David,'' which is not in its dictionary. Obviously, names of people, cities, towns, and words pertaining to certain professions are not in the dictionary. You will be using the word ''David'' a lot, so you will press 2, **Add to dictionary,** as shown in Fig. 2-15.

For the next several words such as ''Foxchase'' and ''Alsoran'' you will press 1, **Word Ok, continue,** because these are names of streets and towns that are seldom used again.

The next word that First Choice stops at is ''jErsey.'' The spelling is right, but it is incorrectly capitalized. A list of possible spellings are suggested as shown in Fig. 2-16. To insert the correct spelling, press 5 **Use Jersey.** The correct spelling is automatically inserted.

The next word the spelling checker stops at is ''Folds'' as shown in Fig.

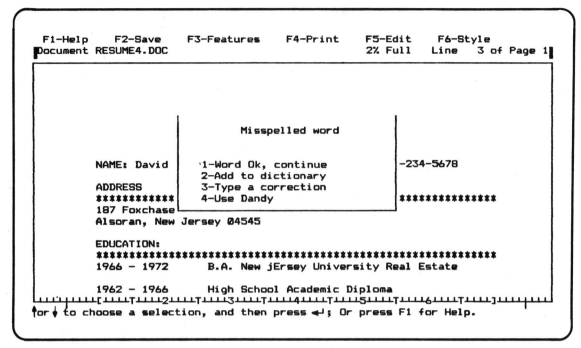

Fig. 2-15. The Spelling Checker Menu.

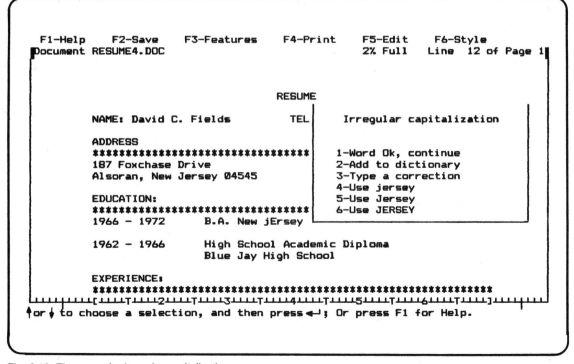

Fig. 2-16. The menu for irregular capitalizations.

2-17. It list a possible spelling, but it is not what you want. Press 3, **Type a correction,** and type in the correct word **Fields.**

The last word the spelling checker stops at is a word that is repeated. In this case, it is "to to" as shown in Fig. 2-18. You want to delete one of the words, so press 2, **Erase repeated word.**

First Choice will also look at words that are punctuated mathematically wrong, such as $23,45.67. When the spelling check is complete, it will say so in a box on the screen. The program will then ask you to press the Return or Enter key to continue.

LISTING THE PERSONAL DICTIONARY

All the words that you add to the dictionary are kept aside in your own personal dictionary. To see your personal dictionary up to this point, go to the Main Menu. Press 5, **Get an existing file.** Type PERSONAL.FC. This is always the name of your personal dictionary. Here you can enter new words, edit words, or delete words. The only word in the dictionary so far is "David."

SEARCHING AND REPLACING TEXT

In your resume you decided that the word "Oil" should be replaced by the word "Utilities." In a short document, you could easily do this by just looking for the word. In a long document, this would be very time-consuming. First Choice has an easy way of doing it.

Press CTRL Home to bring the cursor to the beginning of the document. Press the F3 (Features) key followed by pressing 1, **Find and replace.** You

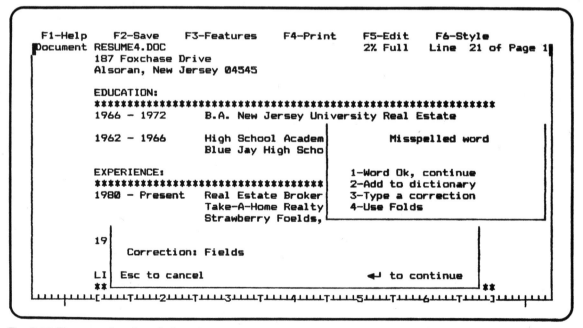

Fig. 2-17. The menu for misspelled words.

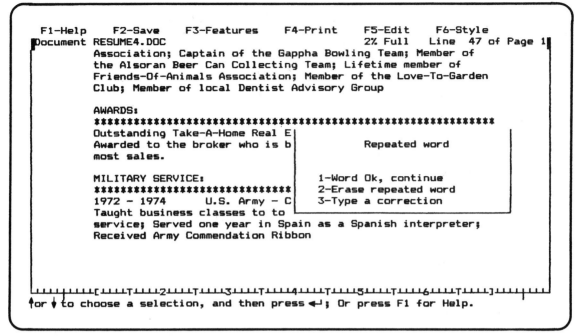

Fig. 2-18. The Repeated Word Menu.

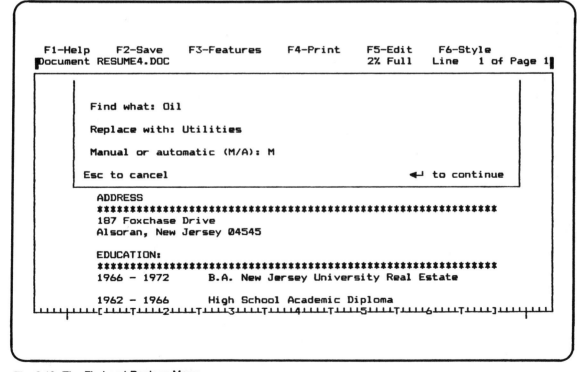

Fig. 2-19. The Find and Replace Menu.

can also use the speed keys Alt F. As shown in Fig. 2-19, type in the word Oil as the word to find. Press the Tab key and type in the word Utilities as the replacement word. You would like to do the replacement manually, so type M. This means that you would like to see each individual replacement, if necessary.

When you press the Return or Enter key, the program will ask you Replace (Y/N). You do want to replace, so type Y. In the Automatic mode, First Choice will automatically replace all the occurrences of Oil by Utilities, whether you want to or not. If there are no more replacements, the program will tell you the number of replacements that it has made.

The final document is shown in Fig. 2-20.

The Find-and-Replace mode is very useful if you are substituting words that are used a lot in a document. For example, you might use the abbreviation of the town ''MP'' for ''Massapequa Park.'' Then all you have to do is find all the MP's and replace them by Massapequa Park.

You can use this feature to jump to any key word in the text by typing in the word you wish to find without typing a replacement word.

ERASING THE WORKING COPY

If you want to erase the document you are presently working on, press the F5 (Edit) key followed by pressing 9, Erase this document.

RETRIEVING A FILE

You would like to retrieve a word processing document that is already saved on your data disk. From First Choice's main menu, select 5, Get an existing file. Figure 2-21 appears, which shows a list of the files on the disk that you can retrieve. To select a file, use the cursor keys to highlight the file you wish to retrieve and press the Enter or Return key. If you are typing in the file name, be sure to include the extension .DOC. This tells First Choice that the file is a word processing document. If your data disk is located in drive B, be sure to type b:RESUME.DOC.

After you press the Return or Enter key, the document will appear on the screen.

LEAVING FIRST CHOICE

You can always leave First Choice by pressing the ESC key from wherever you are and returning to the Main Menu. When you are in the Main Menu, press 8, Leave First Choice. You can also press the down arrow key to highlight that choice, followed by pressing the Return key.

If you have any files that have now been saved, you will be asked if you wish to save them. The files may be saved by pressing the Return key. After the files have been saved, you will exit to *DOS* (the disk operating system). You will then see the A> prompt. You may then turn off your computer or run another program.

```
                           RESUME

    NAME: David C. Fields          TELEPHONE: (201)-234-5678

    ADDRESS
    **********************************************************
    187 Foxchase Drive
    Alsoran, New Jersey 04545

    EDUCATION:
    **********************************************************
    1966 - 1972       B.A. New Jersey University Real Estate

    1962 - 1966       High School Academic Diploma
                      Blue Jay High School

    EXPERIENCE:
    **********************************************************
    1980 - Present    Real Estate Broker
                      Take-A-Home Realty
                      Strawberry Fields, New Jersey

    1974 - 1980       Credit Manager
                      Red Star Utilities Company Cutty Shark, New
    York

    LICENSE:
    **********************************************************
    1972 - New Jersey Brokers License

    OUTSIDE INTERESTS:
    **********************************************************
    Vice-President of the local Strawberry Fields Real Estate
    Association; Captain of the Gappha Bowling Team; Member of
    the Alsoran Beer Can Collecting Team; Lifetime member of
    Friends-Of-Animals Association; Member of the Love-To-Garden
    Club; Member of local Dentist Advisory Group

    AWARDS:
    **********************************************************
    Outstanding Take-A-Home Real Estate Broker for 1985;
    Awarded to the broker who is both civic minded and has the
    most sales.

    MILITARY SERVICE:
    **********************************************************
    1972 - 1974      U.S. Army - Corporal; Quartermaster Corp;
    Taught business classes to servicemen during term of service;
    Served one year in Spain as a Spanish interpreter; Received
    Army Commendation Ribbon
```

Fig. 2-20. The completed resume.

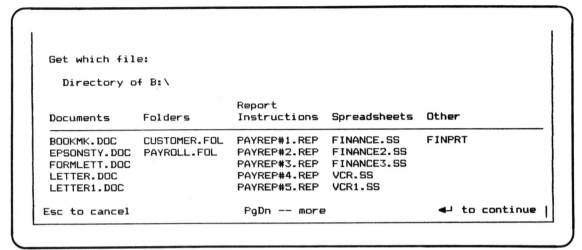

Fig. 2-21. Retrieving a file.

Under no circumstances should you shut the computer off without exiting from the Main Menu. If you do, the document that you were working on would be lost.

SUMMARY

A summary of the commands discussed in this chapter is shown in Fig. 2-22.

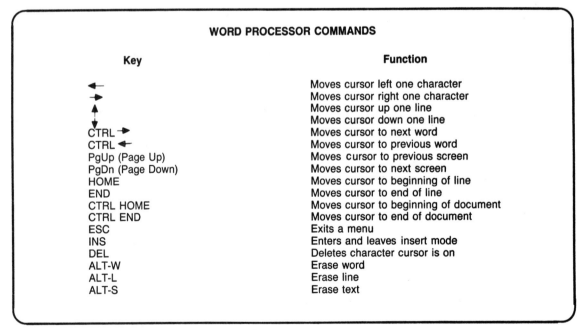

Fig. 2-22. A summary of word processing commands.

Chapter 3

Formatting and Printing Documents

In this chapter, you learn how to format a document by using tabs, indents, headers, and footers. This chapter shows how to change margin and page lengths. Printing styles and printers codes are discussed, including how to right-justify a document. You also learn how to join one or more documents together during the printing process.

BACKGROUND

After all the words have been entered into a document, there is a set of commands that can be used to affect the document's overall appearance. These are usually referred to as *formatting commands*. They include settings for margins, indents, and other characteristics of the document as a whole.

First Choice's word processing module deals with formatting in two major ways. The first way does not do any formatting on the screen, but waits until the document is printed. *Embedded commands* do the formatting. The embedded command is a message to the word processor telling it how to format the document. It is entered onto the screen and is identified using a special symbol (in this case, an asterisk). The word processor will look for indications that a piece of text is not to be treated like others in the document, but rather is to be interpreted as a command. Thus, an embedded command appears on the screen as part of the document, but does not appear in the document that is printed.

The second way of formatting is to format a document on the screen as it is entered, so that you can see exactly what will appear on paper when the document is printed. This kind of formatting is done using commands when the document is created. When the document is printed, it will be reproduced on paper in essentially the same format as it appeared on the screen. You have already seen some of these commands for text that is to be printed in italics, boldfaced, underlined, superscripted, and subscripted. These can be obtained by pressing the F6 (Style) key while you are typing in the document. These styles are normally highlighted on the screen on the characters, words, or paragraphs that possess those particular styles.

When you format a document, you must make decisions about the look of the document—what margins are necessary, whether the material should be indented, whether any information should be centered, and whether the text should appear as a block or with a ragged right edge. First Choice's word processor can handle all of these options.

SETTING AND ERASING TABS

You will now create another word processing document so that you can practice setting tabs and performing other formatting functions. Press 1, **Create a document**, and type in Fig. 3-1.

Notice that the table represented in Fig. 3-1 would be easy to type in if there was a Tab function. This would move the cursor to a particular column every time you pressed the Tab key. First Choice has its own preset tab stops, but you may set as many more as you need. You can even erase the tab stops that come with the program.

To set a tab where the word TABLE begins, go to line 23, column 25 and press F3, **Features**. Press 3, **Set tabs and indent**. Type T to set a tab and press the Enter or Return key to record the tab. If you want to set another tab at the word PRICE, move the cursor to line 23, column 50. Press the F3 (Features) key followed by pressing 3, **Set tabs and indent**. Type T to set a tab and the Enter or Return key to record it. If you want the decimal points to line up, you might have to move the cursor one or two columns to adjust for various amounts of money.

If you want to erase any tab, move the cursor to the T on the ruler at the bottom of the screen where you want the tab deleted. Press the Spacebar to delete the tab, followed by pressing the Return or Enter key.

SETTING AND ERASING INDENTS

Notice that the bottom paragraph of Fig. 3-1 is indented. To indent this paragraph move the cursor to line 36, column 15. Press F3, **Features**, and 3, **Set tabs and indent**. Type i. Notice the appearance of the > sign in the ruler at the bottom of the screen. Press the Enter or Return key to record the indent. The text you type in will be indented, starting at column 15.

To remove the indent, move the cursor to line 42, column 15. Press the F3 key followed by the 3 key. Press the Spacebar to delete the tab followed and press the Enter or Return key.

```
                                    15 Heavenly Drive
                                    Boulder, Colorado 30305

                                    October 15, 1987

Sales Agent
Down Melody Lane Co.
123 FoundIt Drive
Somewhere, New York

Dear Sir:

I am responding to your ad in the Colorado Eagle in regard to
your closing out sale of VCR tapes. For the past several
years, I have been a collector of fine tapes and these will
greatly enhance my collection. Enclose find a check for
$133.93.
Please send me the following tapes:

                    TAPE BUYING LIST

            TABLE                   PRICE
            Gone With the Wine      $69.99
            Best of Rhoda           $29.96
            Shauna & Kathy           $9.99
            Robin Wood              $23.99

                    Total          $133.93

Besides VCR tapes, I am also interested in the following
items that you might have in stock: the first MAD comic book,
a silver plated spoon to commemorate the 1939 World's Fair,
and finally, the first record album by Aunt Teardrops.

        I am a fanatical collector of old comic books, baseball
        cards, record albums, and other trivia, My future goal
        in life is to retire early and become a full time dealer
        in the above. If you have complete collections that you
        have purchased and wish to sell, please contact me
        immediately.

If you have any of the above please contact me immediately.

Sincerely,


Lee J. Unya
```

Fig. 3-1. A sample letter for ordering VCR tapes.

When you are finished typing the document, save it by pressing the F2 (Save) key followed by pressing 1, **Save a copy of this document**. Be sure to give the word processing document an appropriate name such as "VCRTAPES." Again, there is no need to type in the extension .DOC.

MARGIN AND PAGE LENGTH

The word processing module of First Choice provides a variety of commands to control all four margins of the document: top, bottom, left, and right. On normal microcomputer printers, there are 80 characters across the page. Therefore, one inch is equal to 10 characters. If a left margin is one inch wide, it will contain 10 characters.

You will now create another document that will demonstrate the use of margins. From the Main Menu, press 1, **Create a document**, and type in Fig. 3-2. If there is a document in your Working Copy that you wish to remove, press the F5 (Edit) key followed by pressing 9, **Erase this document**. Be sure

```
Dear Mr. Moola:

I am responding to your ad in the March 21st Daily Post
requesting an experience real estate salesperson looking for
advancement. Your ad outlining the additional duties of
computer applications and the opportunity for advancement in
a larger office quickly caught my attention. I am enclosing a
copy of my resume and references may be obtained on request.

For the past several years I have been employed by Mrs.
Mildred Leach as a real estate salesperson with the Take-A-
Home Realty. As you can see from the enclosed resume, I was
voted the Outstanding Real Estate Broker for 1985. I am very
much interested in the uses of computers and the real estate
profession. This includes the uses of computers in loan
qualification. This also includes the development and
application of using house photos in a computerized photo
database.

I look forward meeting you soon. I may be reached at (201)
234-5678 from 10 A.M. to 6 P.M. Monday through Thursday.


Sincerely,


David C. Fields
```

Fig. 3-2. A sample cover letter for a real estate job.

Dear Mr. Moola:

I am responding to your ad in the March 21st Daily
Post requesting an experience real estate
salesperson looking for advancement. Your ad
outlining the additional duties of computer
applications and the opportunity for advancement in
a larger office quickly caught my attention. I am
enclosing a copy of my resume and references may be
obtained on request.

For the past several years I have been employed by
Mrs. Mildred Leach as a real estate salesperson
with the Take-A-Home Realty. As you can see from
the enclosed resume, I was voted the Outstanding
Real Estate Broker for 1985. I am very much
interested in the uses of computers and the real
estate profession. This includes the uses of
computers in loan qualification. This also includes
the development and application of using house
photos in a computerized photo database.

I look forward meeting you soon. I may be reached
at (201) 234-5678 from 10 A.M. to 6 P.M. Monday
through Thursday.

Sincerely,

David C. Fields

Fig. 3-3. A margin change in the real estate letter.

to save this document if you want to. First Choice will always prompt you with
a message saying that the present document in Working Copy has not been
saved and asking if you wish to save it.

If you press F4 (Print), the Margins and Page Length menu will appear.
You can experiment by changing the margins and page lengths to different
lengths. By default ,the normal computer paper is 80 columns. If you are printing on index or rolex cards the page length can be adjusted to whatever you
wish it to be.

Figure 3-3 shows the letter if the left margin is changed to 20. Press the
Tab key to move the cursor from one item to the next and type in the changes

if necessary. An 8 ½ × 11 inch piece of paper contains 66 lines of type. This is about six lines per inch. By default, the Margins and Page Length Menu gives an inch margin at both the top and bottom of the page. If 12 of the 66 lines are used for margins (six at the top and six at the bottom), there are 54 lines that can accommodate the actual text. Try experimenting with different margin and page length settings.

RIGHT JUSTIFICATION

When you print the letter, the left margin is *justified*, or straight, while the right margin is ragged. Right justification makes the edges of text on the right as straight and parallel as those on the left. The text looks like a block. Typical examples of justified text can be found in newspapers or by looking at a text-book. Justification is obtained by inserting some extra blank spaces between the words in the line so that the last word can be pushed out to the right margin.

You can make the right margin justified by answering yes to that particular question in the Print Options menu as shown in Fig. 3-4.

When the letter is printed, it appears as shown in Fig. 3-5. Notice that the left and right margins are straight. This will take the printer a little longer to print because there is more time needed to justify the text.

NEW PAGE AND JOIN COMMAND

You can also combine the printing of two documents together by printing them successively. In the letter you just did, suppose that you wished to attach

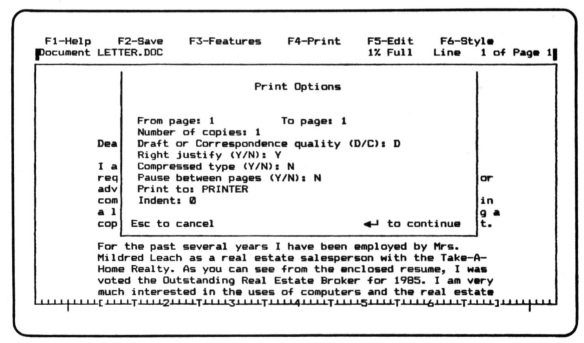

Fig. 3-4. The Print Options Menu—right justification.

Dear Mr. Moola:

I am responding to your ad in the March 21st Daily Post
requesting an experience real estate salesperson looking for
advancement. Your ad outlining the additional duties of
computer applications and the opportunity for advancement in
a larger office quickly caught my attention. I am enclosing a
copy of my resume and references may be obtained on request.

For the past several years I have been employed by Mrs.
Mildred Leach as a real estate salesperson with the Take-A-
Home Realty. As you can see from the enclosed resume, I was
voted the Outstanding Real Estate Broker for 1985. I am very
much interested in the uses of computers and the real estate
profession. This includes the uses of computers in loan
qualification. This also includes the development and
application of using house photos in a computerized photo
database.

I look forward meeting you soon. I may be reached at (201)
234-5678 from 10 A.M. to 6 P.M. Monday through Thursday.

Sincerely,

David C. Fields

Fig. 3-5. Right justification in the real estate letter.

the resume that was created in the last chapter. Figure 3-6 shows the two
commands that are inserted at the end of the letter. This document is called
LETTER1.DOC.

The first command that is typed is NEW PAGE or N, which is enclosed
within two asterisks. This causes the next document to be printed on the next
page. This command can be used anywhere in a document every time you wish
to have something printed on a new page, such as a chart, figure, etc. In your
situation you don't want part of the resume printed at the bottom of the letter
because it would look awkward.

The second command, Join, which is also enclosed within asterisks, tells
what file to print after the letter is printed. If you are working on a very long
document, each part of that document can be saved separately. It is easier to
work on a small document in terms of readability and editing. If you are writing
a small book, you can save each chapter under a separate name and string them
together when you print them.

```
F1-Help    F2-Save    F3-Features    F4-Print    F5-Edit    F6-Style
Document LETTER1.DOC                              1% Full    Line  14 of Page 1
         much interested in the uses of computers and the real estate
         profession. This includes the uses of computers in loan
         qualification. This also includes the development and
         application of using house photos in a computerized photo
         database.

         I look forward meeting you soon. I may be reached at (201)
         234-5678 from 10 A.M. to 6 P.M. Monday through Thursday.


         Sincerely,


         David C. Fields


         *NEW PAGE*

         *JOIN B:RESUME.DOC*


           [    T    2    T    3    T    4    T    5    T    6    T    ]
                 Press F1 for Help; Or, press Esc for the Main Menu.
```

Fig. 3-6. The New Page and Join commands.

```
F1-Help    F2-Save    F3-Features    F4-Print    F5-Edit    F6-Style
Document LETTER2.DOC                              1% Full    Line   1 of Page 1

                         Margins and Page Length menu

         Paper length (in lines): 66
         Left margin: 10                    Right margin: 70
         Top margin: 6                      Bottom margin: 6

         Header (Left,Center,Right): C      Style (None,Underline,Bold): N
         Line 1: Job Application
         Line 2: Real Estate

         Footer (Left,Center,Right): C      Style (None,Underline,Bold): N
         Line 1: November 1987
         Line 2: Page *1*

         Esc to cancel                                 ⏎ to continue

             voted the Outstanding Real Estate Broker for 1985. I am very
             much interested in the uses of computers and the real estate
           [    T    2    T    3    T    4    T    5    T    6    T    ]
```

Fig. 3-7. Setting headers, footers and page numbers.

```
                    Job Application
                     Real Estate


Dear Mr. Moola:

I am responding to your ad in the March 21st Daily Post
requesting an experience real estate salesperson looking for
advancement. Your ad outlining the additional duties of
computer applications and the opportunity for advancement in
a larger office quickly caught my attention. I am enclosing a
copy of my resume and references may be obtained on request.

For the past several years I have been employed by Mrs.
Mildred Leach as a real estate salesperson with the Take-A-
Home Realty. As you can see from the enclosed resume, I was
voted the Outstanding Real Estate Broker for 1985. I am very
much interested in the uses of computers and the real estate
profession. This includes the uses of computers in loan
qualification. This also includes the development and
application of using house photos in a computerized photo
database.

I look forward meeting you soon. I may be reached at (201)
234-5678 from 10 A.M. to 6 P.M. Monday through Thursday.


Sincerely,


David C. Fields
```

```
                   November 1987
                     Page 1
```

Fig. 3-8. A job application with a header and a footer.

```
        This line demonstrates BoldFace print.


     This line demonstrates the Underline style.


     This line demonstrates the Superscript style.


     This line demonstrates the Subscript style.
```

Fig. 3-9. Print styles.

You would now like the document RESUME inserted into the document LETTER1. The file RESUME.DOC is located on drive B:. Notice that the Join command takes place when the two documents are printed. It differs from the Merge command mentioned in the last chapter because the Merge command actually merges the two documents together in the Working Copy. The Join

```
 F1-Help    F2-Save    F3-Features    F4-Print    F5-Edit    F6-Style
Document EPSONSTY.DOC                       0% Full    Line   6 of Page 1
                DEMONSTRATION OF PRINTER CODES FOR EPSON FX-85

     *P 14* Printer Code for Double Width *P 20*

     *P 15* Printer Code for Condensed *P 18*

     *P 27,69* Printer Code for Emphasized Print *P 27,70*

     *P 27,83,1* Printer code for Subscripts *P 27,72,27,84*

     *P 15,27,71* Condensed / Double Strike *P 18,27,72*

     *P 27,87,1,27,71* Double Width / Double Strike
     *P 27,87,0,27,72*

     *P 27,87,1,27,69* Double Width / Emphasized
     *P 27,87,0,27,70*



|....|....[....T....2....T....3....T....4....T....5....T....6....T....]....|....|
                 Press F1 for Help; Or, press Esc for the Main Menu.
```

Fig. 3-10. Embedded print commands.

command is also used if two documents cannot be placed in the Working Copy together because of their size.

SETTING HEADERS AND FOOTERS

Suppose you would like to place a header and footer at the top and bottom of each page. Press the F3 (Features) key and press 4 **Set margins and page length.** Figure 3-7 appears.

Press the Tab key to go from one item to the next and enter the required information. Headers will be printed at the top of each page and, in this case, they will be centered. Footers will be printed at the bottom of each page and each page will be numbered starting with page 1 as shown in Fig. 3-8.

If you want the first page or cover page to be printed without a page number, footer, or header, type **Page *0*.** If you have several cover pages that you do not wish numbers printed on, you can use negative numbers. For example, **Page *-2*** will result in the first three pages not having a page number on

```
          DEMONSTRATION OF PRINTER CODES FOR EPSON FX-85


     Printer  Code  for  Double  Width


Printer Code for Condensed


     Printer Code for Emphasized Print


       Printer code for Subscripts


Condensed / Double Strike



          Double  Width  /  Double  Strike



          Double  Width  /  Emphasized
```

Fig. 3-11. A demonstration of printer codes.

FORMATTING COMMANDS	
Key	**Function**
NEW PAGE or *N*	Causes document to be printed on next page.
JOIN	Combines two documents at printing time.
Page *1*	Each page will be numbered starting with #1.
Page *−1*	First two pages will not be numbered.
	The third page will be numbered starting with #1.

Fig. 3-12. A summary of formatting commands.

it. (DON'T FORGET—the numbers −2, −1, and 0 will cause the word processor NOT to print page numbers).

Headers and footers will only appear on pages that have a page number with a positive number. They would not be printed on the first three pages in this example.

PRINT STYLES & PRINTER CODES

As mentioned in the last chapter, by pressing the F6 (Style) key, you can use the different print styles that are available if your printer can print them. Figure 3-9 shows the output of four of the print styles after the document is run.

Another way of introducing print styles in a document is by the use of printer codes. These codes are normally found in the back of your printer manual. These codes are different for each printer. Figure 3-10 demonstrates several of the codes for an Epson FX-85 printer.

The code at the beginning of the sentence turns the feature on, while the code at the end of the sentence turns it off. Make sure that you place a space after the letter P or PRINTER and that the long codes are not split across two lines. The output to the program is shown in Fig. 3-11.

SUMMARY

A summary of the formatting commands discussed in this chapter is given in Fig. 3-12.

Chapter 4

Creating a Customer File, Mailing Labels, Form Letters and Simple Reports

In this chapter you create a file, add data to it, and learn how to search it for selected information. Once the file is created, you learn how to create mailing labels and form letters from information in it. Creating simple reports from that file, and saving and printing these reports, is also discussed.

BACKGROUND

The primary role of the File module of First Choice is to provide an easy way to create and maintain files and retrieve data from those files for use in developing information.

A *file* is a collection of information organized so that it is easy to retrieve or add data. A telephone directory is an example of a file. Another example of a file is a list of customers that patronize a local VCR tape store. Figure 4-1 shows the structure of the file that you will create in the next section.

Each of the items that is listed in Fig. 4-1 is called a *field*. Each field is capable of holding information about one part of a transaction or business event. A field is a piece of information. Some of the fields in this example are Last Name, First Name, Address, City, State, and Zip. Notice that there is no data located in the form. This will be entered at a later time.

The set of all of the fields that relate to one customer is called a *record*. A record is a set of information about one object, person, etc. A group of records is called a *file*. A file is a collection of organized information.

What you want to have, then, is a file of customers. Information about one

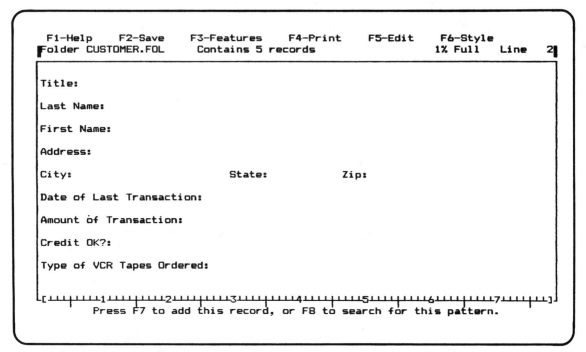

```
   F1-Help    F2-Save     F3-Features    F4-Print    F5-Edit    F6-Style
  Folder CUSTOMER.FOL      Contains 5 records              1% Full   Line   2

 Title:

 Last Name:

 First Name:

 Address:

 City:                    State:            Zip:

 Date of Last Transaction:

 Amount of Transaction:

 Credit OK?:

 Type of VCR Tapes Ordered:


 L⊢⊥⊥⊥|⊥⊥⊥⊥1⊥⊥⊥⊥|⊥⊥⊥2⊥⊥⊥⊥|⊥⊥⊥3⊥⊥⊥⊥|⊥⊥⊥⊥4⊥⊥⊥⊥|⊥⊥⊥5⊥⊥⊥|⊥⊥⊥6⊥⊥⊥⊥|⊥⊥⊥7⊥⊥⊥|⊥⊥J
         Press F7 to add this record, or F8 to search for this pattern.
```

Fig. 4-1. Creating a customer file.

a record. A record can be further broken down into fields. This will be a little clearer when you start to type in the information into the file.

The File module lets you store information in a way that enables it to be easily updated, searched, sorted, retrieved, or printed out. Examples of files would be a mailing list, home or business inventory, a stock market portfolio, etc.

PLANNING A FILE

The first step in planning a file is determining how it will be used. Changes can always take place in a file, but it is better to put as much planning as possible in the initial creation of the file. Changes take a lot of time and can create many avoidable errors.

The first thing to determine is what information you need to store. In other words, what are the fields needed to create the various files? In the VCR store example, you would determine what forms are filled out manually, what records are kept, what data is collected but never used, and what data is missing that you wish you had. The names of the fields or pieces of data that you wish to collect is of extreme importance. Planning now will make life much easier later on.

The next item you need to address is how the information is going to be used. You want to store the names of the customers that patronize the VCR store. Will you create mailing labels that show the customer's first name first? Will the mailing labels be sorted by zip code to help save money in a bulk mailing? Will notices be sent out of all customers who haven't paid their bills within the last thirty days? If you are sorting by last name, you cannot combine the first name, middle initial, and last name in one field. It would be impossible to sort on that combined field.

Could other information be derived from the data entered? For example, could a total bill be calculated if the price per item were entered along with the quantity of that item?

Which fields or data will be required in every record and which will be optional? Try to group required information at the beginning of the record and optional information at the end.

You might find it helpful to design your file on paper before you type it into the machine. Although this step might seem unnecessary, it can save time and trouble later.

CREATING A FILE

You are now an owner of a VCR tape store and would like to create a file of all the customers who ordered tapes so you can create a mailing list and send out form letters announcing new sales. From the Main Menu, press 2, **Create A file folder**. A blank form will appear. You will enter the field names into the form as shown in Fig. 4-1. Notice that the folder or file is called CUSTOMER. It is followed by the extension .FOL. This extension tells you that you are using a folder, not a document. The extension is not added until you save your file. A file name can be up to eight characters in length.

Type in the names of the fields or items directly on the screen. The names of the fields should represent or be associated with the data that is going into each one of them. What you are creating or what you see on the screen is the design of what First Choice calls *forms*. They are comparable to index cards or other methods of inventory keeping. In your store you would like to keep track of the names and addresses of people, the date and amount of their most recent sales, and other information.

The field names can be typed anywhere on the screen. The form does not contain any actual data but just the names of the items that will be entered at a later time. You should leave enough space so the data can be entered. The field name can be up to 2,000 characters in length, and must end with a colon. This signifies the end of the field and tells where the information will be entered at a later time. Once you position one field on the screen, reposition the cursor, type in the field name ending with a colon, etc.

The form should be easy to understand so that data can be entered with no confusion. The title—Mr., Mrs., Ms., Dr.—of the person is entered as a separate field because you wish to use that field in the creation of mailing labels.

A lot of thought goes into the creation of a form and the way a form is laid out. Fields can be changed, added, or deleted at a later time, but it is very time-consuming to do this. The more effort and thought that is put in the creation of a form, the less aggravation there will be later on. You can also check for the spelling of the field names of a form by pressing CTRL Home and accessing the spelling checker through the Features menu.

Once you have finished designing a form, press the F10 key, which saves the design. You have now created the structure of the file. All the field names will be highlighted and you are now ready to enter data into the forms.

ADDING DATA TO A FORM

If you wish to add data to a form at this time, press the F7 key as shown in the bottom of Fig. 4-1. All you have to do is enter data into the form as shown in Fig. 4-2. When you are finished typing data in one form, check to make sure it is correct and press the F10 key to continue adding data to the next record.

Use the Tab key to advance from one field name to the next. Use the Shift Tab keys to go back to the previous field. If you make a mistake, use the Del or arrow keys to correct the data. You can also use the F5 Edit key to erase the information in the field. Figure 4-3 shows the five records that are in the file.

As mentioned before, information about one particular person or item is called a record. A collection of all the records is called a file. In this case it is a customer file.

The information in any field can be of any type. It may consist of *text* such as names, addresses, city, state; *numbers* such as integers, real (numbers with decimal points), money, telephone numbers, social security numbers; or *dates*. Dates must be typed in the form YY/MM/DD, especially if you want to sort on that particular field. The year must be typed in first, followed by the month and the day.

If you run out of space typing in data, press the Ins key and First Choice will expand the field so you can finish typing in your data.

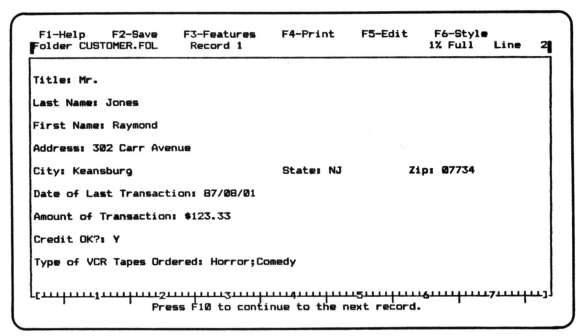

Fig. 4-2. Data entry for the customer file.

CUSTOMER FILE

Title	Last Name	First Name	Address	City	State	Zip
Miss	Waszy	Joann	174 Fox Chase Drive	Delran	NJ	08075
Mrs.	Rich	Rhoda	5363 S. Huron St.	Littleton	CO	80120
Dr.	Smith	Stanley	493 Pollyann Terrace	Paramus	NJ	07652
Ms.	Duke	Joan	266 156 Avenue N.E.	Bellevue	WA	98007
Mr.	Jones	Raymond	302 Carr Avenue	Keansburg	NJ	07734

Last Name	Date of Last Transaction	Amount of Transaction	Credit OK?
Waszy	87/05/17	$100.54	Y
Rich	87/01/05	$55.75	N
Smith	87/03/15	$154.55	Y
Duke	86/12/20	$88.45	Y
Jones	87/08/01	$123.33	Y

Last Name	Type of VCR Tapes Ordered
Waszy	Children;Adventure;Horror
Rich	Animal;Financial;Mystery
Smith	Comedy;Mystery;Adventure
Duke	Medical;Horror
Jones	Horror;Comedy

Fig. 4-3. Complete data for the customer file.

SEARCHING FOR DATA

After the data is entered, you can then search the data to find particular records. Figure 4-4 shows that you wish to find all records of people who purchased more that $100 of VCR tapes and whose interest is in horror movies.

The entry ..horror.. in the field Types of VCR Tapes Ordered is a search for those letters anywhere in the field. When you press the F8 (Search) key, the first record that possesses those characteristics will be displayed on the screen as shown in Fig. 4-5.

If you press the F10 key, the next record that satisfies those conditions will be found. After all the records have been found that satisfy those conditions, First Choice will display how many records were found. In this case there was two.

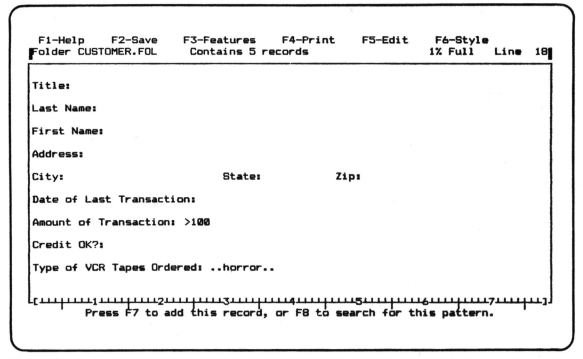

Fig. 4-4. The Search command using inequality and a string.

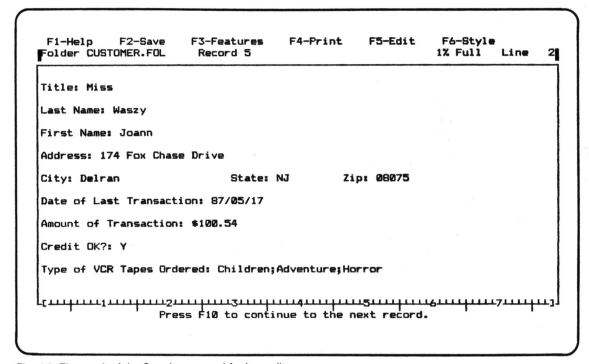

Fig. 4-5. The result of the Search command for inequality.

You can search any field and in any combination of fields. Figure 4-6 shows another search. The search D??e in the Last Name field represents a wildcard search. Each question mark represents a single character. This search could bring up Duke, Duce, Date, or any other words in the file that start with a D and end with an e.

The 86/../.. in the Date of Last Transaction field says that the transaction must have occurred during the year 1986. When you press the F8 key to execute the search, Fig. 4-7 appears. Notice that it is the only record in the file that satisfies these two criteria.

Figure 4-8 shows a search criteria that utilizes the \ (backslash) symbol, which signifies *not*. In this search, you are using /NY in the State field to search for any customer whose state is not New York and whose credit is okay. When the search is executed, the program will find five people who satisfy these requirements.

Figure 4-9 gives several other examples of possible searches. Remember that they could be used alone or in conjunction with several other conditions. Try experimenting with different ideas for searches that you might have.

MAILING LABELS

You now have a file of the names and addresses of all your customers, along with other information about them. You have an upcoming sale and would like the program to generate mailing labels along with form letters. In this section, you learn how to generate mailing labels.

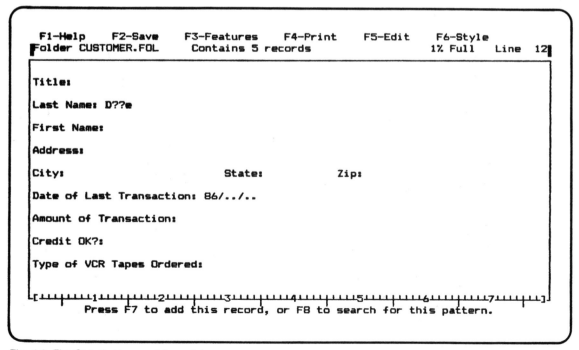

Fig. 4-6. The Search command for a date.

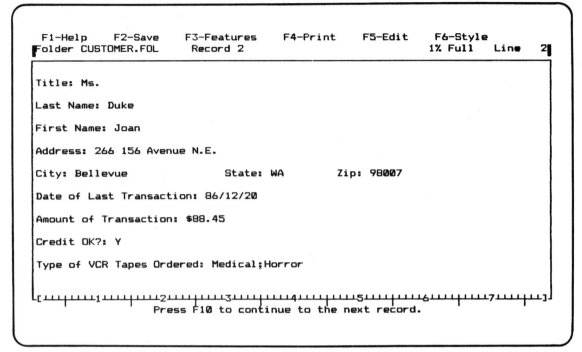

```
   F1-Help    F2-Save    F3-Features    F4-Print    F5-Edit    F6-Style
  Folder CUSTOMER.FOL       Record 2                  1% Full   Line   2

  Title: Ms.

  Last Name: Duke

  First Name: Joan

  Address: 266 156 Avenue N.E.

  City: Bellevue            State: WA        Zip: 98007

  Date of Last Transaction: 86/12/20

  Amount of Transaction: $88.45

  Credit OK?: Y

  Type of VCR Tapes Ordered: Medical;Horror

 [++++++++1++++++++2++++++++3++++++++4++++++++5++++++++6++++++++7++++++++]
            Press F10 to continue to the next record.
```

Fig. 4-7. The result of the Search command for a date.

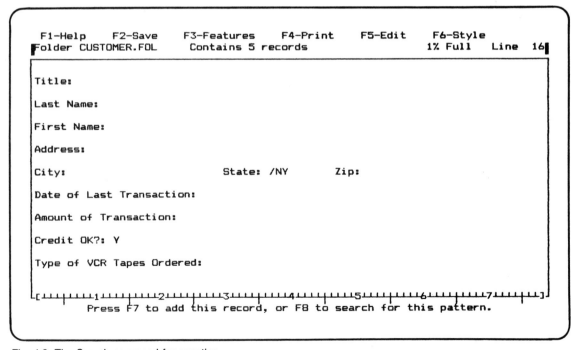

```
   F1-Help    F2-Save    F3-Features    F4-Print    F5-Edit    F6-Style
  Folder CUSTOMER.FOL     Contains 5 records           1% Full   Line  16

  Title:

  Last Name:

  First Name:

  Address:

  City:                     State: /NY       Zip:

  Date of Last Transaction:

  Amount of Transaction:

  Credit OK?: Y

  Type of VCR Tapes Ordered:

 [++++++++1++++++++2++++++++3++++++++4++++++++5++++++++6++++++++7++++++++]
      Press F7 to add this record, or F8 to search for this pattern.
```

Fig. 4-8. The Search command for negation.

Search	Meaning	Examples
>$1,000	find numbers greater than $1,000	$1,111 $10,987
=$1,000	finds entry equal to $1,000	$1,000
<$1,000	finds entry less than $1,000	$999 $454
/ <$1,000	finds entry greater than or equal to $1,000	$1,000 $2,000
/ . .	finds any entries that are empty	
/ . . er	finds any entries that do not end in "er"	Bob Jane
Jbird	finds any entry containing "Jbird"	Jbird
. .	finds fields that have entries	John Bruno
. . zy	finds any entry ending in "zy"	Waszy
Was . .	finds any entry beginning with "Was"	Waszy
. . uk . .	finds any entry that contains a "uk"	Duke fluke
87/ . . / . .	any entry that contains 1987	87/12/30 87/01/02
?aid	finds a four letter entry ending in "aid"	said maid
dat?	finds four letter entry beginning with "dat"	date data
w??e	finds a four letter entry beginning with a "w" and ending with an "e"	wire were

Fig. 4-9. A summary of Search command options with examples.

To create mailing labels, you must create a document that shows the forms of the mailing labels as shown in Fig. 4-10. Type the names of the fields directly on the screen after you press 1, **Create a document**, from the Main Menu.

The field names can be printed anywhere on the screen, but they should be placed in the order that you want them printed. The asterisks around the field names indicate that the information will be obtained from another file. In this case, it will be the CUSTOMER.FOL. The field names printed here are the same field names that are used in the CUSTOMER.FOL.

The data that is in the file will be extracted from that file and placed into the document. After the mailing label document is typed in, press the F3 (Features) key and 4, **Set margins and page length**, to change the margins as shown in Fig. 4-11. Notice that paper length is set to six lines because this is the common length of mailing labels. Also notice that the top and bottom margin lengths are set to zero. This is NOT mentioned in the First Choice manual.

```
        *Title* *First Name* *Last Name*
        *Address*
        *City*, *State* *Zip*
```

Fig. 4-10. A document for mailing labels.

To print the labels, press the F4 (Print) key followed by 3, **Print form letters or labels**. The Print Options menu appears and asks you for the name of the folder that you wish to use. In this case, you wish to obtain records from DOCUMENT.FOL. Type that name in and press Return or Enter. A blank record appears on the screen asking you if you wish to search for any particular records. Because you want all mailing labels of all the records in the file to be printed, press the F10 key. The output is shown in Fig. 4-12.

FORM LETTERS

Just as you created mailing labels in the previous section, you can create a form letter that inserts the names, addresses, city, state, and zip code into the letter. You can also include the field Amount of Transaction in the body of the letter. Type the document shown in Fig. 4-13 and save it as FORMLETT.DOC. Type in the letter directly on the screen after you press 1, **Create a document**, from the Main Menu.

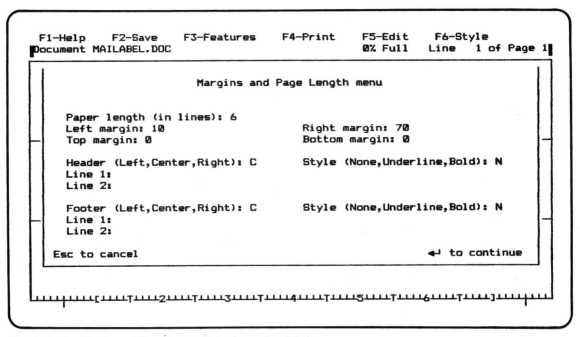

```
 F1-Help    F2-Save    F3-Features    F4-Print    F5-Edit    F6-Style
 Document MAILABEL.DOC                            0% Full    Line   1 of Page 1

                     Margins and Page Length menu

        Paper length (in lines): 6
        Left margin: 10                  Right margin: 70
        Top margin: 0                    Bottom margin: 0

        Header (Left,Center,Right): C    Style (None,Underline,Bold): N
        Line 1:
        Line 2:

        Footer (Left,Center,Right): C    Style (None,Underline,Bold): N
        Line 1:
        Line 2:

     Esc to cancel                                ↵ to continue
```

Fig. 4-11. The Margin and Page Length Menu for mailing labels.

```
Miss Joann Waszy
174 Fox Chase Drive
Delran, NJ 08075



Mrs. Rhoda Rich
5363 S. Huron St.
Littleton, CO 80120



Dr. Stanley Smith
493 Pollyann Terrace
Paramus, NJ 07652



Ms. Joan Duke
266 156 Avenue N.E.
Bellevue, WA 98007



Mr. Raymond Jones
302 Carr Avenue
Keansburg, NJ 07734
```

Fig. 4-12. A print out of the mailing labels.

Figure 4-13 shows the fields that are going to be transferred from the folder CUSTOMER.FOL enclosed in asterisks. Notice that some fields can be repeated twice such as Last Name. The Title field gives a nice touch to the letter. The field Amount of Transaction is embedded in the body of the letter.

To print the letter, press the F4 (Print) key followed by pressing the 3 key, **Print form letters or labels.** The Print Options menu appears. Press the Return or Enter key to continue. A blank form of the record from the CUSTOMER.FOL appears. The program allows you to do a search on the data if needed. Because you want to send a letter to all the people in the data file, press the F10 key. Be sure there is paper in the printer. The form letters will now be printed.

The first form letter is shown in Fig. 4-14. All the fields have been integrated in the letter with all the spacing adjusted. First Choice will adjust the spacing to allow for long or short names and addresses.

```
*First Name* *Last Name*
*Address*
*City*, *State* *Zip*

Dear *Title* *Last Name*:

Enclose find a copy of our catalog showing the latest VCR
movie tapes with their prices. We pride ourselves with our
fast service and in-depth stock.

The sale that we have going on now will last for one month.
If you act now, being a previous customer, will give you an
additional 10% discount from our everyday low prices.

We thank you for your last order of *Amount of Transaction*
and look forward to your order.


Sincerely yours,



Melba P. Grover
```

Fig. 4-13. A document for form letters.

CREATING SIMPLE REPORTS

Once the information is in the file folders, reports can be produced to describe the information. This information can be sorted and arranged in convenient formats.

You will create a simple report which prints out information in the Customer file. To begin, press 3, **Create a report**, from the Main Menu. You must then tell First Choice which folder you are using, which is CUSTOMER.FOL. The extension .REP tells you that you are accessing a report, not a document or a folder. The extension is placed on the report file name after it has been saved. Do not place the extension .REP on the report file name. The program will automatically do so.

You may create many reports for the same folder. Reports can be saved just as documents or folders are. The first report that you wish to create will have the following fields: Last Name, First Name, Date of Last Transaction, and Amount of Transaction.

All fields do not have to be listed in each report. You can select any fields you want in any order that you want. Any report can have up to 20 columns.

Joann Waszy
174 Fox Chase Drive
Delran, NJ 08075

Dear Miss Waszy:

Enclose find a copy of our catalog showing the latest VCR
movie tapes with their prices. We pride ourselves with our
fast service and in-depth stock.

The sale that we have going on now will last for one month.
If you act now, being a previous customer, will give you an
additional 10% discount from our everyday low prices.

We thank you for your last order of $100.54 and look forward
to your order.

Sincerely yours,

Melba P. Grover

Fig. 4-14. The first printed form letter.

```
                         Print Options

    Print totals only (Y/N): N        Pause between pages (Y/N): N

    Print to: PRINTER

    Lines per page: 66                 Page width: 80

    Compressed type (Y/N): N

    Draft or Correspondence quality (D/C): D

    Esc to cancel                               ↵ to continue
```

Fig. 4-15. The print options for summary totals.

The first thing you must do is decide is tell First Choice how to print the report. The Print Options menu is displayed in Fig. 4-15.

You can print totals only, which means you can have a summary report print the results of the calculations but no record itself. You can choose to pause between pages, which means you can use single sheets of paper instead of continuous printer paper. Printing can be to the screen, printer, or a disk file. The lines per page can be changed if you are using different-size computer paper. The width of the paper can be changed if you have wide paper as 132. The whole report can be printed out using compressed type, assuming your printer has this capability. You can also print in draft or correspondence quality, if your printer has this capability. After you are finished with the Print Options Menu, press the Return or Enter key.

SELECTING FIELDS

As mentioned before, you can choose certain fields that can be printed in the report, as shown in Fig. 4-16.

In this case, you wish to have the field Last Name as the first column to be printed in the report, so type a 1. The field First Name will be the second column printed in the report, so type a 2. Continue typing the other two numbers in the report, as shown in Fig. 4-16. Remember to press the Tab key to go from one field to the next and the Shift-Tab key combination to go back to the previous field. When you are finished selecting the columns to be printed, press the F10 key.

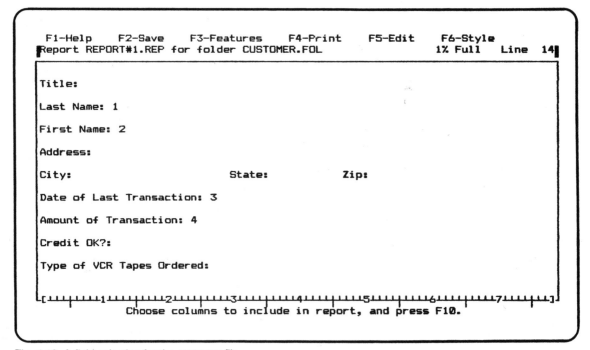

Fig. 4-16. A field selection for the customer file.

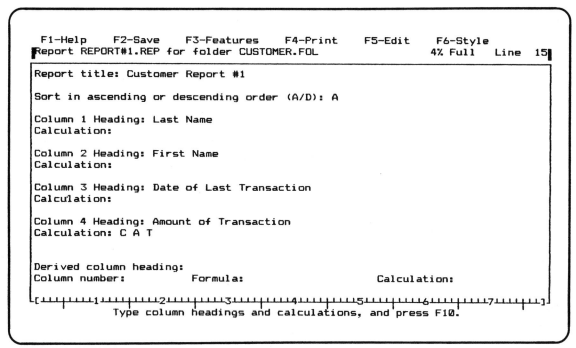

```
  F1-Help     F2-Save     F3-Features     F4-Print     F5-Edit     F6-Style
 Report REPORT#1.REP for folder CUSTOMER.FOL                    4% Full    Line   15

 Report title: Customer Report #1

 Sort in ascending or descending order (A/D): A

 Column 1 Heading: Last Name
 Calculation:

 Column 2 Heading: First Name
 Calculation:

 Column 3 Heading: Date of Last Transaction
 Calculation:

 Column 4 Heading: Amount of Transaction
 Calculation: C A T


 Derived column heading:
 Column number:         Formula:                Calculation:
[┴┴┴┴┴┴1┴┴┴┴┴┴2┴┴┴┴┴┴3┴┴┴┴┴┴4┴┴┴┴┴┴5┴┴┴┴┴┴6┴┴┴┴┴┴7┴┴┴┴┴┴]
           Type column headings and calculations, and press F10.
```

Fig. 4-17. The heading and calculations form.

HEADINGS AND CALCULATIONS

The next screen that appears is the Heading and Calculations form, as shown in Fig. 4-17.

In the report title, type in the name that you wish to give to the report which, in this case, is Customer Report #1. Sorting takes place in First Choice reports in reference to the information in column 1. The sorting can be done in either ascending or descending order. You would like to sort by the field Last Name in alphabetical order, so there is an A in that row. If there are last names that happen to be the same, then the information in the second column is sorted. Press the Tab key until you arrive at the Calculation row in the column 4 Heading: Amount of Transaction. You notice that there are three letters typed in: C A T. This tells First Choice that you wish to count and print out the number of transactions, you wish to compute the average of all the amounts of transactions, and you wish to find the total amount of transactions. These three values will be printed out at the end of the report.

First Choice can also do many other calculations, including subcounts, subaverages, subtotals, new page, and invisible columns. These are discussed in the First Choice manual and will be illustrated in the next chapter where more difficult reports will be shown.

The letters C A T may be typed with no spaces, as CAT. **DO NOT** place commas between the letters or you will get an error message on the screen. When you are finished, press the Return or Enter key and the Selection Menu will appear as shown in Fig. 4-18.

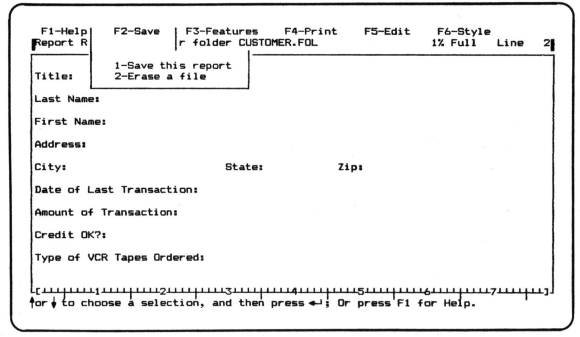

Fig. 4-18. The selection report form.

You can type in the selection criteria if you wish. This is used to select only certain records. If you wish to have all records printed in this report, press the Return or Enter key.

SAVING REPORTS

You can also save the report any time until the time you print it. As shown in Fig. 4-18, you can save the report by pressing the F2 (Save) key. Press the Return or Enter key and give the report a name.

```
                        Customer Report #1

Last Name       First Name      Date of Last Transaction    Amount of Transaction
---------       ----------      ------------------------    ---------------------
Duke            Joan            86/12/20                                    88.45
Jones           Raymond         87/08/01                                   123.33
Rich            Rhoda           87/01/05                                    55.75
Smith           Stanley         87/03/15                                   154.55
Waszy           Joann           87/05/17                                   100.54

                                                            ---------------------
                                            Average:                       104.52
                                            Total:                         522.62
                                            Count:                             5
                                                            ---------------------
```

Fig. 4-19. The printed customer report.

```
   F1-Help    F2-Save    F3-Features    F4-Print|  F5-Edit  | F6-Style
  Report REPORT#2.REP for folder CUSTOMER.FOL    |            4% Full   Line  11

 Report title: Customer Report #2          1-Select text
                                           2-Cut out selected text
 Sort in ascending or descending order (   3-Copy selected text to clipboard
                                           4-Move selected text to clipboard
 Column 1 Heading: Last Name               5-Paste from clipboard
 Calculation:                              6-Insert a blank line
                                           7-Erase this line
 Column 2 Heading: First Name              8-Erase this word
 Calculation:                              9-Erase this record

 Column 3 Heading: Date of Last Transaction
 Calculation:

 Column 4 Heading: Amount of Transaction
 Calculation:


 Derived column heading:
 Column number:          Formula:                    Calculation:
 L[_____1_____2_____3_____4_____5_____6_____7_____]
 ↑or ↓to choose a selection, and then press ↵; Or press F1 for Help.
```

Fig. 4-20. The changed column headings.

```
   F1-Help    F2-Save    F3-Features    F4-Print    F5-Edit    F6-Style
  Report REPORT#2.REP for folder CUSTOMER.FOL              4% Full   Line  15

 Report title: Customer Report #2

 Sort in ascending or descending order (A/D): A

 Column 1 Heading: Last Name
 Calculation:

 Column 2 Heading: First Name
 Calculation:

 Column 3 Heading: Date
 Calculation:

 Column 4 Heading: Amount
 Calculation: C A T


 Derived column heading:
 Column number:          Formula:                    Calculation:
 L[_____1_____2_____3_____4_____5_____6_____7_____]
        Type column headings and calculations, and press F10.
```

Fig. 4-21. The edited column headings.

```
                 Customer  Report  #2

    Last  Name      First  Name       Date        Amount
    ----------      ----------      --------      -------
    Duke            Joan            86/12/20         88.45
    Jones           Raymond         87/08/01        123.33
    Rich            Rhoda           87/01/05         55.75
    Smith           Stanley         87/03/15        154.55
    Waszy           Joann           87/05/17        100.54

                                    ----------------------
                                    Average:  104.52
                                    Total:    522.62
                                    Count:         5
                                    ----------------------
```

Fig. 4-22. The output from the edited column headings.

PRINTING REPORTS

After the selection screen disappears, the report is automatically printed to the screen, printer, or disk as you specified in the print options. The printed report is shown in Fig. 4-19.

Notice the report title, the column headings, and the totals below the Amount of Transaction column.

CHANGING COLUMN HEADINGS

In Fig. 4-19, the third and forth column headings are quite long. The column headings are normally taken from the field names, but you can change or edit them to your liking. Figure 4-20 shows REPORT#2.REP being edited.

The edited headings are shown in Fig. 4-21. The output with the edited headings is shown in Fig. 4-22.

Notice that, because the headings are shortened you may include another column or two in the output. Compare the output in Fig. 4-22 with Fig. 4-19 to see the change in format.

To edit the heading of a report, go to the Headings and Calculations Menu and change the headings by using the Del, Backspace, speed keys, or F5 (Edit) keys. As shown in Fig. 4-20, you can use the F5 key to delete a word by pressing 8, **Erase this word**. You can also use the speed keys ALT W to delete a word in the heading.

Chapter 5

Payroll Problem: Complex Reports

This chapter reviews file creation using a payroll file, and shows how to change its form design. The progression is from simple to complex reports that contain invisible columns, derived columns, subcounts, subaverages, and subtotals. You learn how to produce summary reports, and how to generate new columns from information that is in previous columns.

CREATING A PAYROLL FILE

To create a file which calculates total pay for the week, go to the Main Menu of First Choice and press 2, **Create a file folder**. The fields are shown in Fig. 5-1. Remember from the last chapter that you are creating the *structure* of the file. These are the names of the fields in the folder in which data will be entered. Make sure that you end each field with a colon. Do not worry about the row and column numbers. The form should, simply, be uncluttered and easy to read.

CHANGING THE FORM DESIGN

If, at any time, you would like to add a field, change a field name, erase or move a field, you can do this by pressing the F3 (Features) key as shown in Fig. 5-2. You would then press 4, **Change form design**. It is always a good idea to make a backup of the disk with the reports on it in case you want to revert back to the original report at a later date.

Changing the design should be rarely done. It is highly advisable to plan the field names and format before the file is created. If data is entered into the

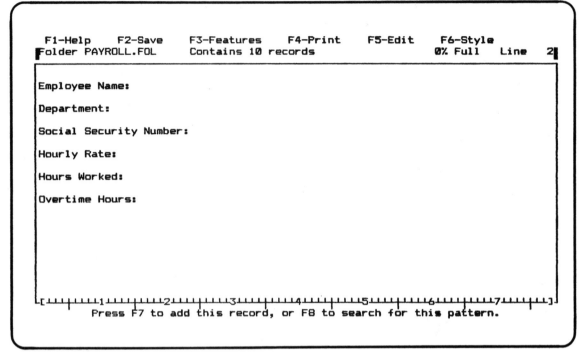

Fig. 5-1. The creation of the payroll folder.

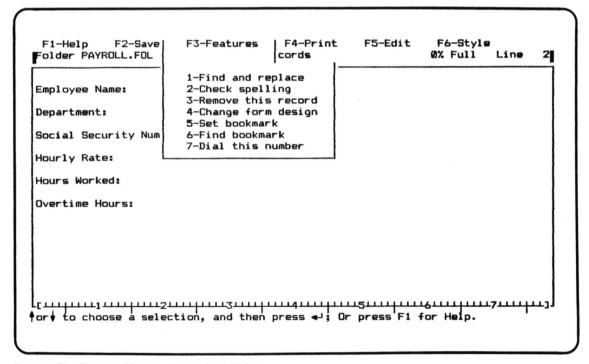

Fig. 5-2. The Features Menu to change form design.

file and the form design is changed, considerable time is wasted when the file is reorganized.

Press 4, **Change form design**, as shown in Fig. 5-3. Depending on what you want to do, press the appropriate key and follow the instructions that First Choice gives you. It is better to change the form design before the data is added to the form. Otherwise, considerable time will be wasted.

If you want to add a field to your form, press 1, **Add fields**. Move the cursor to where you want the new field to be inserted and type the new field name, followed by a colon. When you are finished, press the F10 key to save the changes. All the records will now be updated. If data had been previously added to the file, each record will appear on the screen showing the new field.

If you want to change the name of the field, press 2, **Change field names**. Place the cursor over the name of the field that you wish to change and just type over it, ending with a colon. Press the F10 key to save the new name. If you need more space for the new name, be sure to enter the insert mode by pressing the Ins key to create more space. All the data that was associated with the old field name will now be associated with the new name.

If you want to erase a field, place the cursor over the field that you wish to erase and press 3, **Erase fields**. Press the F10 key to save the changes that you just made. All the data that is associated with that field will now be erased. Do not erase a field that will be used in a calculation at a later point. Otherwise, you will get erroneous results.

If you want to move a field around, press 4, the **Move fields** key. Place the cursor in the position that you want the new field to be placed and type

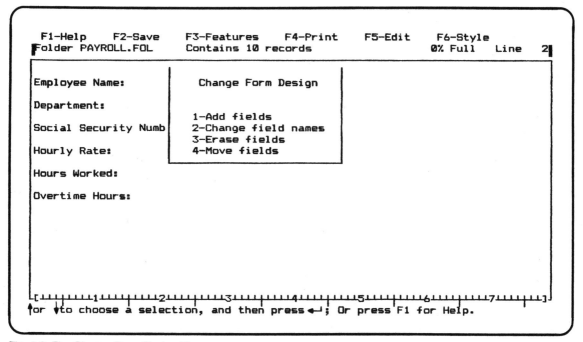

Fig. 5-3. The Change Form Design Menu.

field name exactly as it is in the form, ending with a colon. When you do this, the old field name will disappear. Press the F10 key to save the changes. The records will now be rearranged. No data will be lost because the position of the field has only been moved.

After you have finished entering the field names, press the F10 key to save the form design. You are now ready to enter the data. The first record that is entered is shown in Fig. 5-4.

The complete set of data for the payroll file is shown in Fig. 5-5.

Type the data in. After you fill in each record with data, press the F10 key to save the information. After you have finished typing in the data, save the file by pressing the F2 (Save) key and give it a name such as "PAYROLL.FOL." Don't forget that you do not have to type in the extension .FOL. The program will automatically insert it when it is saved on the disk.

SAVING A RECORD

A single record can be saved so that it can be inserted in a document by pressing the **Save a copy of this record** key from the Save Menu. You will then give the record a file name. This record can now be inserted in any word processing document or sent to another computer using the communications module of First Choice.

IMPORTING DATA

It is unfortunate that data from other programs such as Lotus 1-2-3 and dBASE III PLUS cannot be sent directly into the files of First Choice. First Choice handles data files differently than some of the more popular programs, so direct data transfer simply cannot be done.

CREATING A SIMPLE REPORT

Creating a report involves taking information from a folder or file, sorting and arranging it according to your needs, and displaying and/or printing the results in a table-like format that you design. Reports can also do calculations on a column of numbers. In this section, you create a simple payroll report and keep expanding it to make it a little bit more complex.

Go to the Main Menu and press 3, **Create a report**. Figure 5-6 shows the report with the columns that are to be printed.

Notice that the report always states which folder it is using. In this case, the folder is PAYROLL.FOL. It is possible to use the same report on several different folders. For example, a company may produce a report for each of its branches. The information in each of its branches would be different, but the report format would be the same.

In this report, the field Department would be the first column printed, Employee Name would be the second column printed, Hourly Rate would be the third column printed, and Overtime Hours would be the fourth and last field printed. As you can see, all the fields of a file do not have to be printed. The fields Social Security Number and Hours Worked are in the file, but will not be printed.

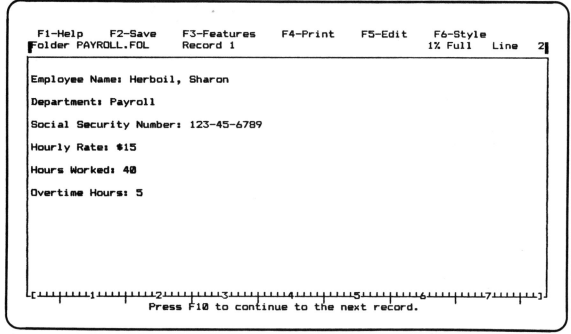

Fig. 5-4. The first data record entered into the payroll file.

PAYROLL DATA FILE

Employee Name	Department	Social Security Number	Hourly Rate
Krawiec, Agnes	Payroll	012-33-4453	$16.00
Duke, Joan	Accounting	049-44-6792	$12.90
DiToro, Hank	Computer	077-34-6528	$17.00
Deluge, Rita Marie	Accounting	012-55-2987	$15.00
DeTrinis, Vincent	Accounting	023-45-7621	$14.00
Muldoon, Diane	Payroll	112-31-1423	$14.60
Fields, David	Computer	014-56-7654	$19.50
Wasniewski, JoAnn	Computer	011-34-4321	$12.00
Bruno, Caroline	Accounting	023-44-6319	$11.50
Herboil, Sharon	Payroll	123-45-6789	$15

Employee Name	Hours Worked	Overtime Hours
Krawiec, Agnes	40	4
Duke, Joan	40	11
DiToro, Hank	40	7
Deluge, Rita Marie	40	0
DeTrinis, Vincent	40	4
Muldoon, Diane	40	3
Fields, David	40	10
Wasniewski, JoAnn	38	0
Bruno, Caroline	40	0
Herboil, Sharon	40	5

Fig. 5-5. The complete payroll data file.

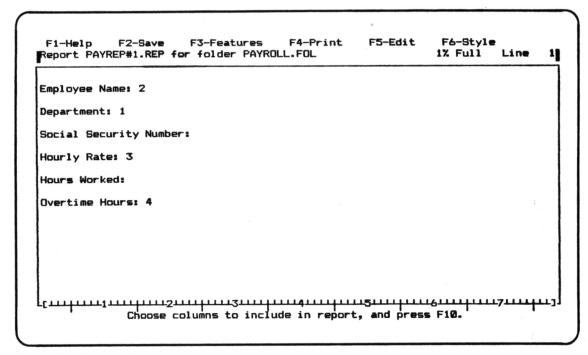

Fig. 5-6. The first payroll report.

You can choose any fields you want to be printed, in any order that you wish. In some cases, it is impractical to print all the fields because of the paper width. There are not enough columns to print all the information across the page.

After pressing the F10 key, the Heading and Calculation Menu appear. Type in the report title as shown in Figure 5-7. The report will be run in ascending order based on the field Department. When you are finished typing in the headings, press the F10 key.

Because you want to print all the data in the file, press the F10 key to start the printing of the report, which is shown in Fig. 5-8. Notice that the report is printed in ascending order by department.

DUPLICATE FIRST COLUMN ENTRIES

Figure 5-8 shows that the department is printed in column 1 only once. If you would like the department to be printed every time, start numbering the columns with the number two as shown in Fig. 5-9.

When you press the F10 key, notice that there is no column 1 as shown in Fig. 5-10. Type in the report title, **Payroll Report #2**.

When you are finished typing in the headings, press the F10 key. Because you want to print all the data in the file, press the F10 key to start the printing of the report, which is shown in Fig. 5-11. Notice that the report is printed in ascending order by department, but the department name is printed each time. Compare Fig. 5-11 and Fig. 5-8 to see the differences.

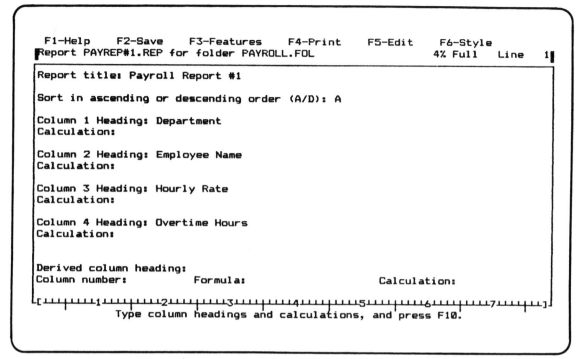

Fig. 5-7. The report titles.

Fig. 5-8. The output for the first payroll report.

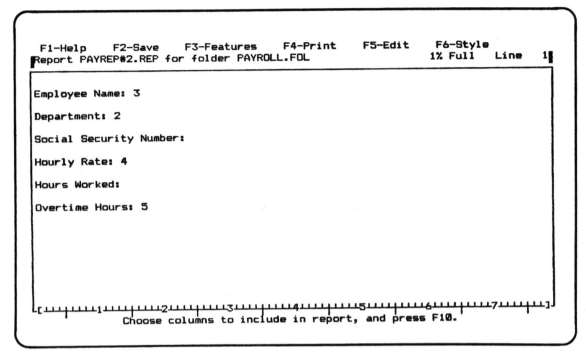

Fig. 5-9. Duplicate first column entries.

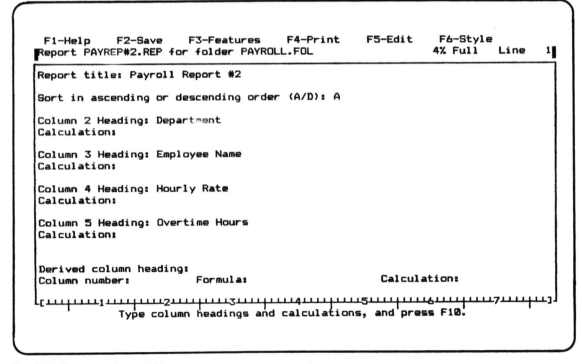

Fig. 5-10. The second report title.

```
                    Payroll Report #2

Department         Employee Name        Hourly Rate      Overtime Hours
----------         -------------        -----------      --------------
Accounting         Deluge, Rita Marie   $15.00           0
Accounting         Duke, Joan           $12.90           11
Accounting         Bruno, Caroline      $11.50           0
Accounting         DeTrinis, Vincent    $14.00           4
Computer           Wasniewski, JoAnn    $12.00           0
Computer           DiToro, Hank         $17.00           7
Computer           Fields, David        $19.50           10
Payroll            Krawiec, Agnes       $16.00           4
Payroll            Muldoon, Diane       $14.60           3
Payroll            Herboil, Sharon      $15             5



Esc-Cancel              There is more to print.           ↵ to continue
```

Fig. 5-11. The output for the second payroll report.

DERIVED COLUMNS

Suppose that you would now like to create and print a column from the information that is entered in the payroll file. Figure 5-12 shows the fields that will be used to create this report. You would like to create and print out a column that calculates a field Total Pay which is based on how many hours a person works in a week.

The Heading and Calculations Menu shows how this is done as shown in Fig. 5-13.

The report title is typed in, "Payroll Report—Derived Column." The fields Hourly Rate, Hours Worked, and Overtime Hours have the letter N in the calculation field. You do not have to type these in. First Choice automatically places them in those fields based on the data that was entered into the file. All of these fields contain numeric data, so an N is placed in them. These fields are used in the formula for Total Pay.

The field Total Pay is a derived column heading. This field did not originally exist in the payroll file but is calculated from the three previous fields: Hourly Rate, Hours Worked, and Overtime Hours. If you look in the column headings in Fig. 5-13, you will notice that each column has a number next to it. The field Hourly Rate is column 2. The field Hours Worked is column 3. The field Overtime Hours is column 4. These column numbers are the numbers referred to in the formula for the new derived field, Total Pay. This new field is in the fifth column

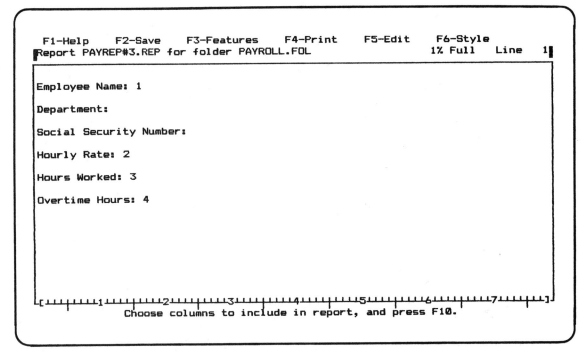

Fig. 5-12. The third payroll report.

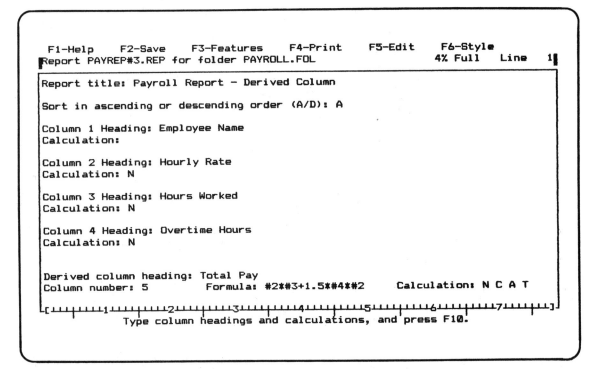

Fig. 5-13. The Headings and Calculations Menu with formula.

and is called Total Pay. Look at the formula for calculating the Total Pay. The formula is:

#2*#3 + 1.5*#4*#2

The first part of the formula says to multiply the contents of the Hourly Rate (column 2) by the contents of Hours Worked (column 3). The number sign (#) is used to identify the columns. This part of the formula gives the regular pay for working forty hours or less.

The rest of the formula computes the overtime pay. It says to multiply 1.5 (time-and-a-half for overtime pay) times the Overtime Hours (column 4) times the Hourly Rate (column 2). If you add these two numbers together—the regular pay plus the overtime pay—you will obtain the total pay for the week.

You may use any of the four arithmetic operations, addition (+), subtraction (−), multiplication (*), and division (/), as well as parentheses to create a formula. If you run out of room while typing the formula, press the Ins key to enter the insert mode and continue typing. Expressions in parentheses are evaluated first, followed by multiplication and division, followed by addition and subtraction.

In the calculation row of Total Pay you see the following letters: N C A T. This says that the field is numeric (N), that you wish to count how many records there are (C), that you wish to compute the average total pay (A), and that you wish to compute the total of all the salaries (T). Remember that it is not necessary to type in the letter N; First Choice automatically put it in. There is no need to place spaces between the letters. For example, you could enter NCAT. **DO NOT** place commas between the letters. This will give you an error.

When the report is run, the output should look like Fig. 5-14. Notice the count, average, and total are printed at the bottom of column 5, Total Pay. If First Choice cannot compute the answer, it will print a series of asterisks as an answer. This tells you that you might be dividing by zero or the number is too long to be calculated and printed.

INVISIBLE COLUMNS

A Heading and Calculation screen is shown in Fig. 5-15. Compare Fig. 5-13 with Fig. 5-15. They are almost exactly the same except for the report title and the letter I which is used in Fig. 5-15 in the calculations of columns 2, 3, and 4. This says that the headings are invisible. They are used in the calculation of the formula for the total pay, but they will not be printed out in the final report.

The formula to calculate Total Pay is based on the three columns Hourly Rate, Hours Worked, and Overtime Hours, but these columns will not be printed. The output of the report is shown in Fig. 5-16.

Compare Fig. 5-16 with Fig. 5-14. The two reports are almost exactly the same except that three columns are not printed in Fig. 5-16 because First Choice considers them invisible. Invisible columns are very useful to use if you can only print a few columns in a report because of your printer capabilities.

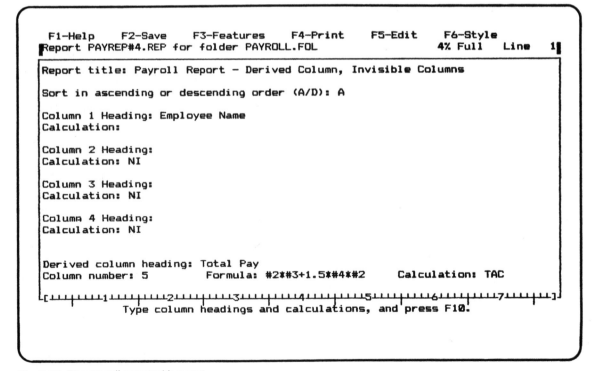

```
                    Payroll Report - Derived Column

  Employee Name       Hourly Rate   Hours Worked   Overtime Hours   Total Pay
  --------------      -----------   ------------   --------------   ---------
  Bruno, Caroline        11.50          40              0            460.00
  Deluge, Rita Marie     15.00          40              0            600.00
  DeTrinis, Vincent      14.00          40              4            644.00
  DiToro, Hank           17.00          40              7            858.50
  Duke, Joan             12.90          40             11            728.85
  Fields, David          19.50          40             10          1,072.50
  Herboil, Sharon        15.00          40              5            712.50
  Krawiec, Agnes         16.00          40              4            736.00
  Muldoon, Diane         14.60          40              3            649.70
  Wasniewski, JoAnn      12.00          38              0            456.00

                                                      -----------------------
                                                      Average:      691.81
                                                      Total:      6,918.05
                                                      Count:            10
                                                      -----------------------


  Esc-Cancel               There is more to print.        ⏎ to continue
```

Fig. 5-14. An output report with a derived column.

```
    F1-Help     F2-Save     F3-Features     F4-Print     F5-Edit     F6-Style
  Report PAYREP#4.REP for folder PAYROLL.FOL               4% Full    Line    1

  Report title: Payroll Report - Derived Column, Invisible Columns

  Sort in ascending or descending order (A/D): A

  Column 1 Heading: Employee Name
  Calculation:

  Column 2 Heading:
  Calculation: NI

  Column 3 Heading:
  Calculation: NI

  Column 4 Heading:
  Calculation: NI


  Derived column heading: Total Pay
  Column number: 5          Formula: #2*#3+1.5*#4*#2       Calculation: TAC
  L[++++|++++1++++|++++2++++|++++3++++|++++4++++|++++5++++|++++6++++|++++7++++|++++]J
                   Type column headings and calculations, and press F10.
```

Fig. 5-15. The payroll report with a sort.

```
       Payroll Report - Derived Column, Invisible Columns

              Employee Name          Total Pay
            ------------------        ---------
            Bruno, Caroline              460.00
            Deluge, Rita Marie           600.00
            DeTrinis, Vincent            644.00
            DiToro, Hank                 858.50
            Duke, Joan                   728.85
            Fields, David              1,072.50
            Herboil, Sharon              712.50
            Krawiec, Agnes               736.00
            Muldoon, Diane               649.70
            Wasniewski, JoAnn            456.00

                                    ------------------
                                    Average:    691.81
                                    Total:    6,918.05
                                    Count:          10
                                    ------------------

 Esc-Cancel              There is more to print.         ↵ to continue
```

Fig. 5-16. The payroll report with a derived column.

SUBCOUNTS, SUBAVERAGES, AND SUBTOTALS

In the last two reports, you did a count, average, and total on one column. Suppose you would like to generate a report that computes the count, average, and total for each department, along with the grand totals for all the departments.

Figure 5-17 shows which columns are to be placed in the report along with the order in which they are to be printed. You will make the field Department the first column, which will be printed in alphabetical order.

Figure 5-18 shows the Heading and Calculation screen that corresponds to this report.

Column 1, the department heading, is not shown because there is no room for it on the screen. There are three invisible columns as before: column 4, Hourly Rate; column 5, Hours Worked; and column 6, Overtime.

Look at the calculation row of the derived column Total Pay. There are six calculations that are to be performed on that particular field. They may be typed in any order.

The letters SC stand for the subcount. Every time there is a change in column 1, Department, a count is printed. The letters SA stand for the subaverage. Every time there is a change in column 1, Department, a subaverage is printed. ST is the subtotal. Every time there is a change in column 1, Department, a subtotal is printed.

The letters SC, SA, and ST will also produce complete counts, complete averages, and grand totals at the end of the report, so there is no need to include

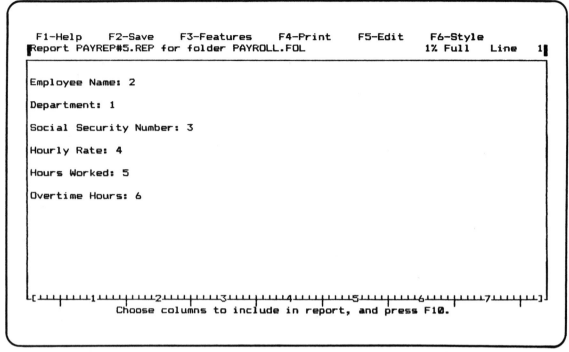

```
   F1-Help     F2-Save     F3-Features     F4-Print     F5-Edit     F6-Style
Report PAYREP#5.REP for folder PAYROLL.FOL              1% Full    Line    1

Employee Name: 2

Department: 1

Social Security Number: 3

Hourly Rate: 4

Hours Worked: 5

Overtime Hours: 6




L[⌊⌊⌊⌊|⌊⌊⌊⌊1⌊⌊⌊⌊|⌊⌊⌊⌊2⌊⌊⌊⌊|⌊⌊⌊⌊3⌊⌊⌊⌊|⌊⌊⌊⌊4⌊⌊⌊⌊|⌊⌊⌊⌊5⌊⌊⌊⌊|⌊⌊⌊⌊6⌊⌊⌊⌊|⌊⌊⌊⌊7⌊⌊⌊⌊|⌊⌊⌊]
            Choose columns to include in report, and press F10.
```

Fig. 5-17. The report with subcounts, subaverages and subtotals.

```
   F1-Help     F2-Save     F3-Features     F4-Print     F5-Edit     F6-Style
Report PAYREP#5.REP for folder PAYROLL.FOL              5% Full    Line   26
Column 2 Heading: Employee Name
Calculation:

Column 3 Heading: Social Security Number
Calculation:

Column 4 Heading: Hourly Rate
Calculation: I

Column 5 Heading: Hours Worked
Calculation: I

Column 6 Heading: Overtime
Calculation: I



Derived column heading: Total Pay
Column number: 7        Formula: #4*#5+1.5*#6*#4     Calculation:C A SC SA ST T

Derived column heading:
L[⌊⌊⌊⌊|⌊⌊⌊⌊1⌊⌊⌊⌊|⌊⌊⌊⌊2⌊⌊⌊⌊|⌊⌊⌊⌊3⌊⌊⌊⌊|⌊⌊⌊⌊4⌊⌊⌊⌊|⌊⌊⌊⌊5⌊⌊⌊⌊|⌊⌊⌊⌊6⌊⌊⌊⌊|⌊⌊⌊⌊7⌊⌊⌊⌊|⌊⌊⌊]
            Type column headings and calculations, and press F10.
```

Fig. 5-18. The Heading and Calculations Menu with invisible columns.

the letters C A T. If included, however, this will not give any errors in the report, as you will soon see.

Notice that the column numbers in the formula for the Total Pay are different because you are including more columns in the report. The formula is the same, but the column numbers are different. The output of the report is shown in Fig. 5-19.

Each department has its own count, average, and total of the field Total Pay along with the count, average, and total of all departments. Every time there is change in department, the subcounts, subaverages, and subtotals are printed out.

```
                  Payroll Report - Subtotals & Totals

Department        Employee Name      Social Security Number     Total Pay
----------        -------------      ----------------------     ---------
Accounting        Bruno, Caroline    023-44-6319                   460.00
                  Deluge, Rita Marie 012-55-2987                   600.00
                  DeTrinis, Vincent  023-45-7621                   644.00
                  Duke, Joan         049-44-6792                   728.85

                                                 Average:         608.21
                                                 Total:         2,432.85
                                                 Count:                4

Computer          DiToro, Hank       077-34-6528                   858.50
                  Fields, David      014-56-7654                 1,072.50
                  Wasniewski, JoAnn  011-34-4321                   456.00

                                                 Average:         795.67
                                                 Total:         2,387.00
                                                 Count:                3

Payroll           Herboil, Sharon    123-45-6789                   712.50
                  Krawiec, Agnes     012-33-4453                   736.00
                  Muldoon, Diane     112-31-1423                   649.70

                                                 Average:         699.40
                                                 Total:         2,098.20
                                                 Count:                3


                                                 -------------------
                                                 Average:         691.81
                                                 Total:         6,918.05
                                                 Count:               10
                                                 -------------------


                              Page 1
```

Fig. 5-19. The subtotals and totals of the output payroll report.

```
                        Print Options

    Print totals only (Y/N): Y        Pause between pages (Y/N): N

    Print to: PRINTER

    Lines per page: 66              Page width: 80

    Compressed type (Y/N): Y

    Draft or Correspondence quality (D/C): D

    Esc to cancel                              ↵ to continue
```

Fig. 5-20. The summary report in the Print Options Menu.

PRINTING TOTALS ONLY—A SUMMARY REPORT

The previous report printed the breakdown for each department. If you would like only the final summaries to be printed, you would create a summary report. A summary report is created by answering Y to the following question:

Print totals only (Y/N):

This question is in the Print Options Menu, as shown in Fig. 5-20.

The summary report is shown in Fig. 5-21. The report and column headings are printed, but only the final statistics are printed.

NEW PAGE

If you would like the information for each department to be printed on a separate page, include the letter P in the calculation row of column 1 as shown in Fig. 5-22.

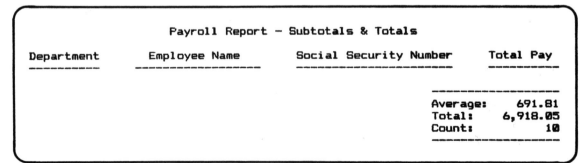

Fig. 5-21. The output payroll summary report.

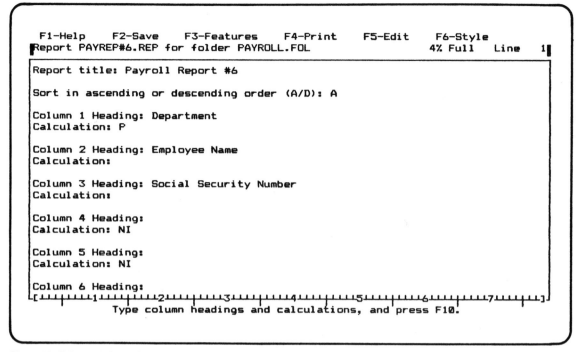

```
   F1-Help     F2-Save     F3-Features     F4-Print     F5-Edit     F6-Style
 Report PAYREP#6.REP for folder PAYROLL.FOL                4% Full   Line   1

 Report title: Payroll Report #6

 Sort in ascending or descending order (A/D): A

 Column 1 Heading: Department
 Calculation: P

 Column 2 Heading: Employee Name
 Calculation:

 Column 3 Heading: Social Security Number
 Calculation:

 Column 4 Heading:
 Calculation: NI

 Column 5 Heading:
 Calculation: NI

 Column 6 Heading:
 [    1      2      3      4      5      6      7    ]
             Type column headings and calculations, and press F10.
```

Fig. 5-22. Printing information on a new page.

Every time there is a change in department, the information about that department will be printed on a separate page as shown in Fig. 5-23. Only the first page of output is shown.

USING TWO DERIVED COLUMNS

First Choice can print up to 20 columns, including three derived columns. These derived columns may or may not be invisible. Suppose you would now like to give each of your employees a bonus of four percent of their total pay. Figure 5-24 shows how this is done.

```
                        Payroll Report #6

 Department          Employee Name         Social Security Number      Total Pay
 ----------          -------------         ----------------------      ---------

 Accounting          Bruno, Caroline       023-44-6319                    460.00
                     Deluge, Rita Marie    012-55-2987                    600.00
                     DeTrinis, Vincent     023-45-7621                    644.00
                     Duke, Joan            049-44-6792                    728.85




                                 Page 1
```

Fig. 5-23. The output of the first page.

Notice that there are two derived columns: Total Pay and Bonus. Total Pay is called column 7 and is based on the three invisible columns Hourly Rate, Hours Worked, and Overtime Hours. The formula is the same one that was used in the previous examples. Not shown in Fig. 5-24, due to lack of room, is the field Department in column 1.

The second derived column heading is called Bonus, and its column number is 8. The formula for column 8 says to multiply the results of column 7 (Total Pay) by 4% to give the bonus pay. Statistics will also be printed on the Bonus field to indicate the count, average, and total bonuses for each department and the grand total.

Derived columns can only be generated from columns that come before or to the left, of them. You cannot create a column that is to contain information from a nonexistent column. The output of this report is shown in Fig 5-25.

Now you can see the total pay and bonuses for each department and the grand totals at the bottom of the report. If you did not want to see the Total Pay column, you could have made it an invisible column by typing an I in the calculation section of column 7.

SAVING, RETRIEVING, AND ERASING REPORTS

Reports can be saved and printed just like any other document or file. Figure 5-24 shows a report PAYREP#7.REP for folder PAYROLL.FOL. The screen will always show the name of the report if it has been saved, along with the

```
   F1-Help    F2-Save    F3-Features    F4-Print    F5-Edit    F6-Style
  Report PAYREP#7.REP for folder PAYROLL.FOL              4% Full    Line    7

  Column 2 Heading: Employee Name
  Calculation:

  Column 4 Heading: Hourly Rate:
  Calculation: NI

  Column 5 Heading: Hours Worked:
  Calculation: NI

  Column 6 Heading: Overtime Hours:
  Calculation: NI


  Derived column heading: Total Pay
  Column number: 7        Formula: #4*#5+1.5*#6*#4        Calculation: STSASC

  Derived column heading: Bonus
  Column number: 8        Formula: #7*.04                 Calculation: STSASC

  Derived column heading:
  [      1       2       3       4       5       6       7      ]
           Type column headings and calculations, and press F10.
```

Fig. 5-24. Two derived columns—total pay and bonus.

```
         Payroll Report #7 - Two Derived Columns

Department         Employee Name        Total Pay        Bonus
------------       ------------------   ----------       -------
Accounting         Bruno, Caroline         460.00         18.40
                   Deluge, Rita Marie      600.00         24.00
                   DeTrinis, Vincent       644.00         25.76
                   Duke, Joan              728.85         29.15

                              Average:     608.21         24.33
                              Total:     2,432.85         97.31
                              Count:            4             4

Computer           DiToro, Hank            858.50         34.34
                   Fields, David         1,072.50         42.90
                   Wasniewski, JoAnn       456.00         18.24

                              Average:     795.67         31.83
                              Total:     2,387.00         95.48
                              Count:            3             3

Payroll            Herboil, Sharon         712.50         28.50
                   Krawiec, Agnes          736.00         29.44
                   Muldoon, Diane          649.70         25.99

                              Average:     699.40         27.98
                              Total:     2,098.20         83.93
                              Count:            3             3


                              ------------------        -------
                              Average:     691.81         27.67
                              Total:     6,918.05        276.72
                              Count:           10            10
                              ------------------        -------
```

Fig. 5-25. Output using two derived columns.

file or folder that it is using. In this case, there are seven different reports for one file or folder.

There is no limit to the number of different reports that can be used with one file or folder. Notice that all reports are saved with the extension .REP, while all files or folders have the extension .FOL.

All reports can be saved before they are printed. You can save a report by pressing the F2 (Save) key followed by pressing 1, **Save this Report**. The

CALCULATION CODES

Abbreviation	Meaning	Explanation
T	TOTAL	Adds all the numbers in the column and prints the results.
ST	SUBTOTAL	Gives a subtotal every time the information in column 1 changes. A grand total is printed at the end.
A	AVERAGE	Prints the average at the end of each column.
SA	SUBAVERAGE	Gives a subaverage each time the data in column 1 changes, and an average of all the numbers at the end.
C	COUNT	Counts how many entries are in that column.
SC	SUBCOUNT	Gives a subcount each time the data in column 1 changes and a complete count at the end.
N	NUMERIC	The entry that is typed in is treated numerically. All text is ignored. All decimals are lined up and trailing zeros are added to format the entries.
P	PAGE	When the data in column 1 changes, a new page is started. Only works in column 1.
I	INVISIBLE	A column where the data is used but not printed. Hence, it is invisible.

Fig. 5-26. A summary of calculation modes.

program will now ask you for the name in which you wish to save this report. Type in the name, but do not type in the extension .REP.

After a report is saved, you can retrieve it as many times as you wish. To obtain a report, go to the Main Menu and press 4, **Get an existing file.** Type in or choose the name of the file that you wish to obtain. You can change any part of the report before you run it, or you can run it as is.

A report, like any other document or file, can be erased by pressing the F2 (Save) key followed by pressing 4, **Erase a file.**

SUMMARY

Figure 5-26 presents a summary of the calculation codes discussed in this chapter.

Chapter 6

Income/Expense Statement Spreadsheets

This chapter discusses what a spreadsheet is, how to create one, and how to use it. You learn how to place row and column headings, values, and formulas into the spreadsheet. Summing cells, changing cell style, and recalculating a spreadsheet are discussed. You also learn how to edit, save, load, and print a spreadsheet.

BACKGROUND

Spreadsheets are very useful in financial applications where large numbers of figures and formulas need to be organized to ensure accuracy. A typical use for a spreadsheet is in budgeting, which requires reports such as income statements and balance sheets. These reports are laid out in columns and rows to create *cells*. Some of these cells contain labels or headings that tell what each figure is. Some cells tell data about a company. Other cells contain figures which are used in calculations to compute the figures in other cells.

A *spreadsheet* provides a column and row layout of information to allow the user to make entries at intersections, or cells. Spreadsheet *layout* refers to the designation of column and row entries. Using a personal computer with 640K, you can have a spreadsheet of up to 1,024 rows and 768 columns. This will give you approximately 18,000 usable calls.

There are four types of entries that can be made in a spreadsheet cell. They are headings, labels, numbers, and formulas or functions. These four entries and their uses are discussed later in this chapter.

Spreadsheets can be used to complete any data calculations and manipulations involving numbers and text that is usually performed with pencil, paper, and calculator. Some uses of spreadsheets are: budget preparation, business modeling, sales forecasting, investment analysis, payroll, taxes, and real estate management. The list is only limited by your imagination.

The spreadsheet software module helps improve your accuracy, efficiency, and productivity. Once a worksheet is prepared, other choices (*"what if"* options) can be easily considered by making the appropriate changes and instructing the spreadsheet to recalculate all entries to reflect these changes. This allows you to forecast the effects on many parts of a business. The spreadsheet recalculates all related cells quickly and accurately. This will allow you to spend more time on making decisions.

CREATING A SPREADSHEET

To create a spreadsheet, from the Main Menu of First Choice, type 4, **Create a spreadsheet,** and press the Return key. A spreadsheet will appear on the screen as shown in Fig. 6-1. The top line shows you the purpose of the function keys. Notice the similarities of the uses of these keys when you created a word processing document, file or folder.

As mentioned in a previous chapter, First Choice is an integrated program. The F1 (Help) key provides help in all three of the functions mentioned so far: word processing, files, and spreadsheets. Notice that the same functions are performed by the same function key in all three of the modules.

```
 F1-Help    F2-Save    F3-Features    F4-Print    F5-Edit    F6-Style
Spreadsheet                                       0% Full   Row   1  Column   1
1024 By 768      C1    C2    C3    C4    C5    C6    C7    C8    C9

 R1
 R2
 R3
 R4
 R5
 R6
 R7
 R8
 R9
 R10
 R11
 R12
 R13
 R14
 R15
 R16
 R17
 R18
           Press F1 for Help; Or, press Esc for the Main Menu.
```

Fig. 6-1. The spreadsheet layout.

The second line from the top of the figure shows the position of the cursor by denoting the row and column number. It also shows how much memory is used up by the spreadsheet. It tells you that the computer that is running this spreadsheet has 640K of memory, because the spreadsheet size is 1024 by 768. On the left side the rows are numbered R1, R2, R3, etc. Across the top are the columns, which are labelled C1, C2, C3, etc.

The intersection of a row and column is called a cell. When you enter a spreadsheet, the cursor is initially on the cell R1C1. All cells are named by the intersection of the row with the corresponding column.

CURSOR KEYS

Try experimenting by moving the cursor around the screen. Use the four arrows, the End key, the Home key, etc. The CTRL Home keys will bring you to the upper left corner of the screen which has the coordinate R1C1 representing the first row and first column. The row and column where the cursor is placed is always shown in the top right corner of the screen below the menu bar.

The Tab key will move the cursor one cell to the right, while the Shift Tab keys will move the cursor one cell to the left. Figure 6-2 shows a summary of all the keys and their cursor movements.

QUICK ENTRY

You will create a spreadsheet that simulates the income and expense statement of a VCR store. The first thing you would like to do is place headings at the top of the screen to represent the four quarters of the year. Headings may be up to 20 characters wide and five lines long. By default, the heading size is six characters long, but First Choice will expand or contract the sizes of the columns depending on the width of the headings.

These headings are to be labelled QTR 1, QTR 2, QTR 3, and QTR 4. To enter the first heading, move the cursor to the cell below C1 and type **QTR 1**. You could very easily type in the rest of the headings in cells C2, C3, and C4 but there is an easy way to do it. Move the cursor to cell R1C1 by pressing the CTRL Home keys. Press the up arrow to go to cell C1. While the cursor is in the cell heading C1, press the F3 (Features) key as shown in Fig. 6-3.

Press 5, **Start Quick Entry**. Move the cursor to cells C2, C3, and C4 by pressing the Tab key. Notice how the original heading, QTR 1, is automatically increased by one. You could have also entered the headings automatically by pressing the ALT Q keys, which are the speed keys that avoid the menus.

The spreadsheet looks like Fig. 6-4. You can tell you are in quick entry by looking at the top center of the screen. To exit the quick entry, press the ESC key.

First Choice can duplicate headings in quick entry that end in a number, such as ''Day 1.'' It also knows how to increment headings that start with Jan, January, Mon, Monday, July 87, etc. All the text, including capitalization, is duplicated.

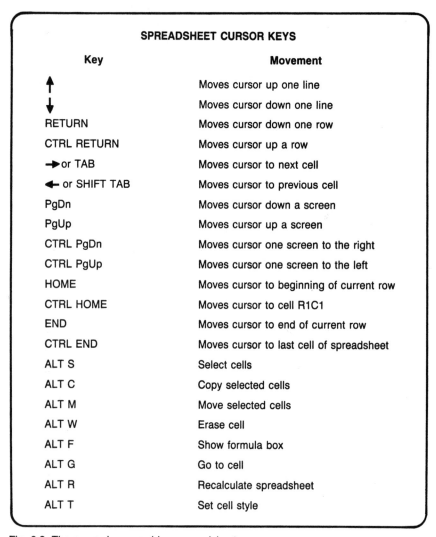

SPREADSHEET CURSOR KEYS

Key	Movement
↑	Moves cursor up one line
↓	Moves cursor down one line
RETURN	Moves cursor down one row
CTRL RETURN	Moves cursor up a row
→ or TAB	Moves cursor to next cell
← or SHIFT TAB	Moves cursor to previous cell
PgDn	Moves cursor down a screen
PgUp	Moves cursor up a screen
CTRL PgDn	Moves cursor one screen to the right
CTRL PgUp	Moves cursor one screen to the left
HOME	Moves cursor to beginning of current row
CTRL HOME	Moves cursor to cell R1C1
END	Moves cursor to end of current row
CTRL END	Moves cursor to last cell of spreadsheet
ALT S	Select cells
ALT C	Copy selected cells
ALT M	Move selected cells
ALT W	Erase cell
ALT F	Show formula box
ALT G	Go to cell
ALT R	Recalculate spreadsheet
ALT T	Set cell style

Fig. 6-2. The cursor keys used in a spreadsheet.

Headings may be erased by pressing the F5 (Edit) key, pressing 1, **Select cells**, and pressing 2, **Erase selected cells** key or 8, **Erase this cell**. A cell can also be erased by pressing the ALT W speed keys.

Row headings, like column headings can be up to 20 characters wide and five lines long. Just as with column headings, First Choice will expand or contract the width of the row heading depending on its length.

To type in the first row heading, INCOME, as shown in Fig. 6-5, press the CTRL Home keys to bring the cursor to R1C1. Press the Shift Tab keys to move the cursor to the first row heading and type in **INCOME**. Move the down-arrow key to the cells below and type in the row headings as shown in Fig. 6-5. If you make a mistake in typing, press the Delete or Backspace keys to make corrections.

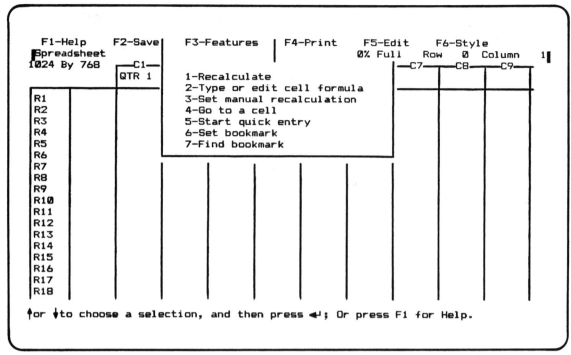

Fig. 6-3. The Features Menu for spreadsheets.

Fig. 6-4. An example of the use of quick entry for headings.

```
 F1-Help     F2-Save    F3-Features    F4-Print    F5-Edit    F6-Style
Spreadsheet                                       0% Full    Row   6   Column    1
    1024 By 768              —C1——  —C2—  —C3——  —C4——  —C5——  —C6——  —C7——
                            QTR 1  | QTR 2 | QTR 3 | QTR 4

R1      INCOME
R2        Credit          11,456.77
R3        Cash             7,645.88
R4        Other              454.22
R5
R6      Total Income
R7
R8.     EXPENSES
R9        Credit Fees
R10       Payroll
R11       Overhead                                              Name:
R12       Product Cost                                          Formula R6C1:
R13       Miscellaneous                                         Total r2c1..r4c1
R14
R15     Total Expense
R16
R17     Profit
R18

Press Esc to cancel changes, or press Alt-F or any cursor key to save changes.
```

Fig. 6-5. Typing row headings.

You are now ready to type in the values. Move the cursor to R2C1 and type in 11456.77. Do not type in the commas. The program will automatically insert commas when you leave the cell. In a similar manner, press the down arrow and type in the values shown for cells R3C1 and R4C1 in Fig. 6-5. Notice that First Choice automatically lines up the data by inserting the commas and lining up the decimal point.

SUMMING CELLS

In cell R6C1, you will type in the formula to add up all the incomes. Press the ALT F keys to show the formula box as shown in Fig. 6-5. You could have also pressed 2, **Type or edit cell formula**, from the F3 (Features) menu. First Choice has many built in formulas that will do certain calculations on cells. Some will compute the absolute value, averages, maximum, minimum, square root, variance, standard deviation, totals, and the use of trigonometric functions.

The word "Total" is called a *keyword* by the program, and it adds the contents of the cells following the keyword. Total can be typed in uppercase or lowercase. All expressions following keywords may be enclosed in parentheses.

Your example says to sum the contents of R2C1, R3C1, and R4C1. All three incomes are added together to give you the total income. Type in the formula as shown. To exit the formula box, press the ALT F keys or the ESC key. As soon as you leave the formula box, the cell is calculated.

Continue entering the values as shown in Fig. 6-6 in the Expenses column. In cell R15C1, there is another sum formula shown in the formula box shown on Fig. 6-6. This formula totals all the expenses. Notice that there is an "at" sign (@) preceding the keyword. This symbol is optional in the formula.

The formula for the profit in R17C1 is **R6C1 − R15C1**. The arithmetic symbols may be used anywhere in the formula itself: + for addition, − for subtraction, / for division, ∗ for multiplication, and ∗∗ or ^ for exponentiation. Notice that as soon as you leave the formula box the profit is calculated.

Figure 6-7 shows the values that may be entered in cells R2C2, R3C2, and R4C2. Also shown in Fig. 6-7 is the Edit Menu which tells you how to erase selected cells, insert rows and columns, insert a row/column, erase a single cell or an entire spreadsheet.

The formula for R6C2 is the same as the formula for R6C1 except for the column number. The formula could be moved from one column to the next by pressing the F5 (Edit) key, pressing 1, **Select cells**, while in the R6C1 cell, pressing 3, **Copy selected cells to clipboard**, moving the cursor to cell R6C2 and pressing 5, **Paste from clipboard**.

In your VCR store example, notice that the payroll for the first three quarters are the same. The quick entry keys can also be used to duplicate values in as many columns as you want. Place the cursor in the cell R10C1 and press the ALT Q keys for quick entry. Press the Tab key twice and notice how the value is duplicated as shown in Fig. 6-8. To exit the Quick Entry mode, press the ALT Q keys or the ESC key.

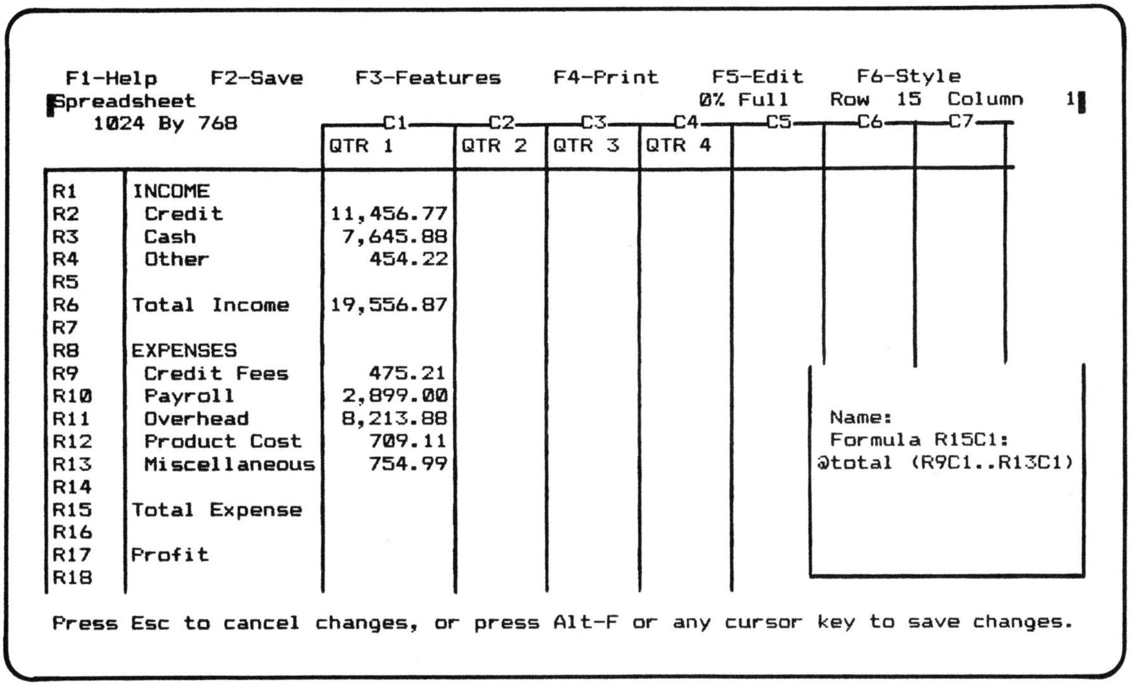

Fig. 6-6. The use of the total function.

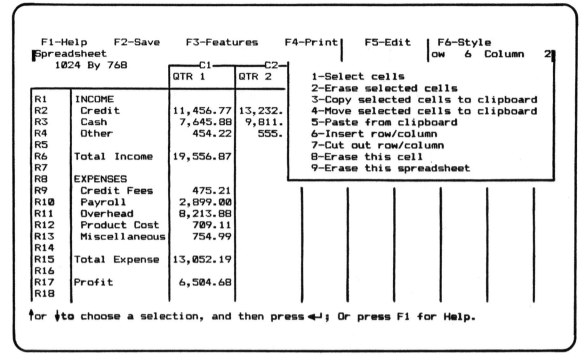

Fig. 6-7. The Edit Menu for spreadsheets.

```
 F1-Help    F2-Save    F3-Features    F4-Print|   F5-Edit  |F6-Style
Spreadsheet                                              |ow   6 Column  2|
    1024 By 768          ——C1——  ——C2—
                          QTR 1    QTR 2    1-Select cells
                                            2-Erase selected cells
 R1      INCOME                              3-Copy selected cells to clipboard
 R2      Credit       11,456.77 13,232.      4-Move selected cells to clipboard
 R3      Cash          7,645.88  9,811.      5-Paste from clipboard
 R4      Other           454.22   555.       6-Insert row/column
 R5                                          7-Cut out row/column
 R6      Total Income 19,556.87             8-Erase this cell
 R7                                          9-Erase this spreadsheet
 R8      EXPENSES
 R9       Credit Fees    475.21
 R10      Payroll      2,899.00
 R11      Overhead     8,213.88
 R12      Product Cost   709.11
 R13      Miscellaneous  754.99
 R14
 R15     Total Expense 13,052.19
 R16
 R17     Profit         6,504.68
 R18

↑or ↓to choose a selection, and then press ↵; Or press F1 for Help.
```

Fig. 6-7. The Edit Menu for spreadsheets.

```
 F1-Help     F2-Save    F3-Features   F4-Print    F5-Edit    F6-Style
Spreadsheet                    Quick Entry        1% Full   Row 10 Column  3|
    1024 By 768         ——C1——  ——C2——  ——C3——  ——C4——  ——C5——  ——C6——  ——C7——
                         QTR 1    QTR 2    QTR 3    QTR 4
 R1      INCOME
 R2      Credit       11,456.77 13,232.00
 R3      Cash          7,645.88  9,811.38
 R4      Other           454.22   555.88
 R5
 R6      Total Income 19,556.87 23,599.26
 R7
 R8      EXPENSES
 R9       Credit Fees    475.21   527.40
 R10      Payroll      2,899.00  2,899.00 2,899.00
 R11      Overhead     8,213.88
 R12      Product Cost   709.11
 R13      Miscellaneous  754.99
 R14
 R15     Total Expense 13,052.19
 R16
 R17     Profit         6,504.68
 R18

        Type first entry and move to next row or column.
```

Fig. 6-8. An example of quick entry for values.

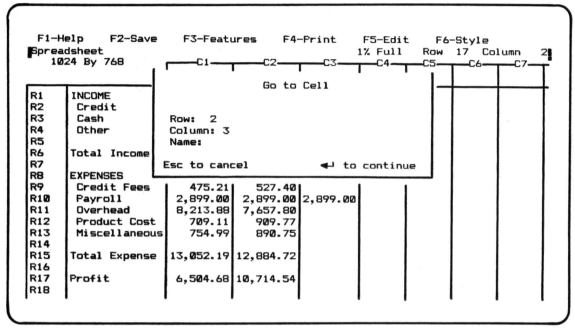

Fig. 6-9. The Go To Cell Menu.

GOTO CELL

The cursor can also be moved quickly about the spreadsheet by pressing the F3 (Features) key and pressing 4, Go to a cell. Figure 6-9 appears. You can type in any row and column that you want or the name of a cell. Naming a cell is discussed in the next chapter.

Figure 6-10 shows the completed spreadsheet. A new column C5, Year Total, is added. All the formulas for rows 6, 15, and 17 are the same for each column.

Comments can be made anywhere in the spreadsheet by just typing them in. The title which starts at R18C2 could have been placed at the top of the spreadsheet, but it would have interfered with the column headings.

Figure 6-11 shows how to add more formulas that are not shown in Fig. 6-10. The average total expenses and the average profit are calculated and printed with a dollar ($) sign. The formula box in Fig. 6-11 shows how the average profit is calculated. The screen cannot possibly show the whole spreadsheet if it contains many columns and rows. You can scroll to the right and bottom of the spreadsheet by using the cursor keys or the other cursor movement keys.

CELL AND GLOBAL STYLE

Dollar signs, currency symbols, percent signs, and number of decimal places can be defined by pressing the F6 (Style) key. Each individual cell or the entire (*global*) spreadsheet can be changed as shown in Fig. 6-12. To change an individual cell, press 1, Set cell style. To change all cells, press 2, Set global

```
 F1-Help    F2-Save    F3-Features    F4-Print    F5-Edit    F6-Style
▌Spreadsheet                                      1% Full   Row   1  Column   1▌
      1024 By 768         ──C1──    ──C2──    ──C3──    ──C4──    ──C5──    ──C6──
                         QTR 1     QTR 2     QTR 3     QTR 4     Year Total

 R1    INCOME
 R2     Credit          11,456.77 13,232.00 13,233.50 14,323.44   52,245.71
 R3     Cash             7,645.88  9,811.38 10,220.00 11,767.00   39,444.26
 R4     Other              454.22    555.88    397.00    441.56    1,848.66
 R5
 R6    Total Income     19,556.87 23,599.26 23,850.50 26,532.00   93,538.63
 R7
 R8    EXPENSES
 R9     Credit Fees        475.21    527.40    528.60    623.77    2,154.98
 R10    Payroll          2,899.00  2,899.00  2,899.00  3,100.00   11,797.00
 R11    Overhead         8,213.88  7,657.80  8,650.00  8,998.44   33,520.12
 R12    Product Cost       709.11    909.77    870.00    987.00    3,475.88
 R13    Miscellaneous      754.99    890.75    933.66    875.00    3,454.40
 R14
 R15   Total Expense    13,052.19 12,884.72 13,881.26 14,584.21   54,402.38
 R16
 R17   Profit            6,504.68 10,714.54  9,969.24 11,947.79   39,136.25
 R18                              VCR INCOME/EXPENSE STATEMENT

        Press F1 for Help; Or, press Esc for the Main Menu.
```

Fig. 6-10. The completed spreadsheet.

```
 F1-Help    F2-Save    F3-Features    F4-Print    F5-Edit    F6-Style
▌Spreadsheet VCR.SS                               2% Full   Row  21  Column   5▌
      1024 By 768         ──C1──    ──C2──    ──C3──    ──C4──    ──C5──    ──C6──
                         QTR 1     QTR 2     QTR 3     QTR 4     Year Total

 R8    EXPENSES
 R9     Credit Fees        475.21    527.40    528.60    623.77    2,154.98
 R10    Payroll          2,899.00  2,899.00  2,899.00  3,100.00   11,797.00
 R11    Overhead         8,213.88  7,657.80  8,650.00  8,998.44   33,520.12
 R12    Product Cost       709.11    909.77    870.00    987.00    3,475.88
 R13    Miscellaneous      754.99    890.75    933.66    875.00    3,454.40
 R14
 R15   Total Expense    13,052.19 12,884.72 13,881.26 14,584.21   54,402.38
 R16
 R17   Profit            4,504.68 10,714.54  9,969.24 11,947             $9,284.06
 R18                              VCR INCOME/EXPENSE STATEME  Name:
 R19                                                          Formula R21C5:
 R20                              Average Total Expense────── @AVG (R17C1..R17C4)
 R21                              Average Profit────────────
 R22
 R23
 R24
 R25

   Press Esc to cancel changes, or press Alt-F or any cursor key to save changes.
```

Fig. 6-11. An example of the use of the average function.

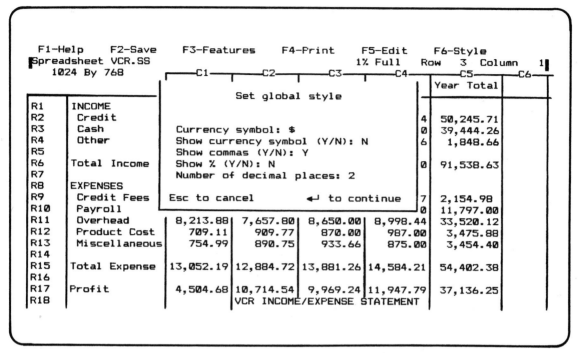

F1—Help   F2—Save   F3—Features   F4—Print   F5—Edit   F6—Style
Spreadsheet VCR.SS   1% Full   Row   3 Column   1

Fig. 6-12. The Set Global Style Menu.

style. The currency symbol, the $ sign, can be displayed with the dollar amount, such as $987.65. The currency symbol can be printed out for each cell or the whole spreadsheet. Other currency symbols for other countries can also be displayed if needed. For example, the symbol FF can be used for the French frank, SFr for the Swiss frank, L for lire, P for peso, Pts for Spanish peseta, and Y for Japanese yen.

Percent signs can be shown, such as 77% and 8.98%. If you are using a number with a percent sign in a formula, it will divide the number by 100. The number of decimal places can be printed out to whatever you want. All numbers will be rounded to the decimal places that you specify, up to 15 places. The default value is two decimal places.

If you specify a style that is too small to hold the number, you will see a series of asterisks in that particular cell. This tells you to increase the number of decimal places in the cell.

WHAT-IF

Now that you have gone through all the effort of making a spreadsheet, of what value is it? If you made a mistake typing any entry, all you have to do is change the cell value and see the changes to the rest of the values that depend on the value. For example, move the cursor to R2C1 and type in the number 9456.77. After you move the cursor out of the cell, all of the cells that relate to it will change. In this case, the total income, profit, and year totals will change.

By typing in various numbers, you can see the "what-if" situation. You can predict how much you can save by reducing payroll, overhead, product cost, etc. You can change any number of values and see the result on the total problem. Remember that you must leave a cell to see a calculation take place.

RECALCULATION

When the spreadsheet is accessed, First Choice puts you in the automatic recalculation mode. This means that every time you make a change in the spreadsheet and leave a cell, the whole spreadsheet will be recalculated. This can be very time-consuming if you have a very large spreadsheet.

If you want to set a manual recalculation, recalculating only if you want to, you must press the F3 (Features) key and then press 3, **Set Manual recalculation.** This can also be accomplished by pressing the quick entry keys, ALT R. Every time you want to recalculate the spreadsheet, press the ALT R keys.

It is highly recommended that, when you are learning to create spreadsheets, you leave the setting on automatic recalculation. It is very easy to forget to recalculate at the end of many changes.

SAVING A SPREADSHEET

To save a spreadsheet, press the F2 (Save) key followed by pressing **1, Save a copy of this spreadsheet.** Give the spreadsheet a name such as VCR and press the Return or Enter key. There is no need to type the extension .SS. The program automatically adds it on when it is saved.

LOADING A SPREADSHEET

To load a spreadsheet, from the Main Menu of First Choice, press 5, **Get an existing file,** and type the name of the file, VCR, followed by pressing the Return or Enter key. This is shown in Fig. 6-13.

As you type in a spreadsheet, experiment to see how the cursor keys, row and column headings, values, and formulas are calculated. Experimentation is the key to success in spreadsheets. Try typing in different headings, values, and formulas to see the changed results.

Notice on the top left of the screen that First Choice places the extension .SS with the file name to indicate that it is a spreadsheet. This figure illustrates the income and expenses statement of a simulated VCR store. Each cell or intersection of row and column on the spreadsheet has a name. The columns headings are at the top of the screen: QTR 1, QTR 2, QTR 3, QTR 4, and Year Total. Each cell has a coordinate that you can go to and access the particular information in the cell. For example, the cell R1C1 has the text INCOME, the cell R6C2 has the number 23,850.50, and the cell R15C5 has the number 54,402.38.

From the Main Menu of First Choice, type 4, **Create a spreadsheet.** You can then type in the column and row headings, the values, and formulas.

```
 F1-Help    F2-Save    F3-Features    F4-Print    F5-Edit    F6-Style
Spreadsheet VCR.SS                              1% Full   Row  3 Column  1
    1024 By 768       ┌──C1───┬──C2───┬──C3───┬──C4───┬──C5───┬──C6──
                      │ QTR 1 │ QTR 2 │ QTR 3 │ QTR 4 │Year Total│
┌────┬────────────────┼───────┼───────┼───────┼───────┼──────────┼────
│R1  │ INCOME         │       │       │       │       │          │
│R2  │  Credit        │ 9,456.77│13,232.00│13,233.50│14,323.44│50,245.71│
│R3  │  Cash          │ 7,645.88│ 9,811.38│10,220.00│11,767.00│39,444.26│
│R4  │  Other         │  454.22│  555.88│  397.00│  441.56│ 1,848.66│
│R5  │                │       │       │       │       │          │
│R6  │ Total Income   │17,556.87│23,599.26│23,850.50│26,532.00│91,538.63│
│R7  │                │       │       │       │       │          │
│R8  │ EXPENSES        │       │       │       │       │          │
│R9  │  Credit Fees   │  475.21│  527.40│  528.60│  623.77│ 2,154.98│
│R10 │  Payroll       │ 2,899.00│ 2,899.00│ 2,899.00│ 3,100.00│11,797.00│
│R11 │  Overhead      │ 8,213.88│ 7,657.80│ 8,650.00│ 8,998.44│33,520.12│
│R12 │  Product Cost  │  709.11│  909.77│  870.00│  987.00│ 3,475.88│
│R13 │  Miscellaneous │  754.99│  890.75│  933.66│  875.00│ 3,454.40│
│R14 │                │       │       │       │       │          │
│R15 │ Total Expense  │13,052.19│12,884.72│13,881.26│14,584.21│54,402.38│
│R16 │                │       │       │       │       │          │
│R17 │ Profit         │ 4,504.68│10,714.54│ 9,969.24│11,947.79│37,136.25│
│R18 │                │       VCR INCOME/EXPENSE STATEMENT        │

        Press F1 for Help; Or, press Esc for the Main Menu.
```

Fig. 6-13. Loading a spreadsheet.

```
 F1-Help    F2-Save    F3-Features │ F4-Print │ F5-Edit    F6-Style
Spreadsheet VCR.SS                 │          │ 1% Full   Row  1 Column  1
    1024 By 768       ┌──C1───┬────│ 1-Print this spreadsheet │tal │──C6──
                      │ QTR 1 │QTR │ 2-Print selected cells only│
┌────┬────────────────┼───────┼────┴──────────────────────────┴────
│R1  │ INCOME         │       │       │       │       │          │
│R2  │  Credit        │11,456.77│13,232.00│13,233.50│14,323.44│52,245.71│
│R3  │  Cash          │ 7,645.88│ 9,811.38│10,220.00│11,767.00│39,444.26│
│R4  │  Other         │  454.22│  555.88│  397.00│  441.56│ 1,848.66│
│R5  │                │       │       │       │       │          │
│R6  │ Total Income   │19,556.87│23,599.26│23,850.50│26,532.00│93,538.63│
│R7  │                │       │       │       │       │          │
│R8  │ EXPENSES        │       │       │       │       │          │
│R9  │  Credit Fees   │  475.21│  527.40│  528.60│  623.77│ 2,154.98│
│R10 │  Payroll       │ 2,899.00│ 2,899.00│ 2,899.00│ 3,100.00│11,797.00│
│R11 │  Overhead      │ 8,213.88│ 7,657.80│ 8,650.00│ 8,998.44│33,520.12│
│R12 │  Product Cost  │  709.11│  909.77│  870.00│  987.00│ 3,475.88│
│R13 │  Miscellaneous │  754.99│  890.75│  933.66│  875.00│ 3,454.40│
│R14 │                │       │       │       │       │          │
│R15 │ Total Expense  │13,052.19│12,884.72│13,881.26│14,584.21│54,402.38│
│R16 │                │       │       │       │       │          │
│R17 │ Profit         │ 6,504.68│10,714.54│ 9,969.24│11,947.79│39,136.25│
│R18 │                │       VCR INCOME/EXPENSE STATEMENT        │

 ↑or ↓to choose a selection, and then press ←┘; Or press F1 for Help.
```

Fig. 6-14. The Print Menu for a spreadsheet.

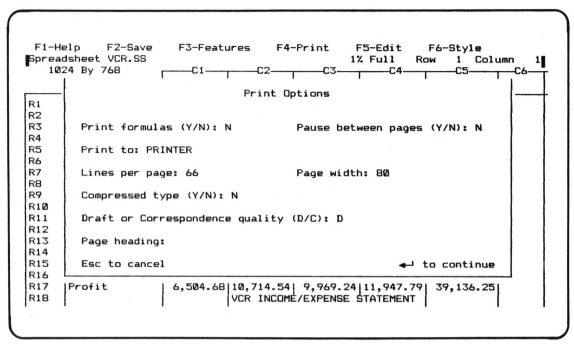

```
   F1-Help      F2-Save     F3-Features     F4-Print      F5-Edit     F6-Style
  Spreadsheet VCR.SS                              1% Full    Row   1  Column   1
     1024 By 768        ┌──C1──┬──C2──┬──C3──┬──C4──┬──C5──┬──C6──┐
 ┌──────────────────────────────────────────────────────────────────────┐
 │R1 │                        Print Options                               │
 │R2 │                                                                    │
 │R3 │  Print formulas (Y/N): N          Pause between pages (Y/N): N      │
 │R4 │                                                                    │
 │R5 │  Print to: PRINTER                                                 │
 │R6 │                                                                    │
 │R7 │  Lines per page: 66               Page width: 80                   │
 │R8 │                                                                    │
 │R9 │  Compressed type (Y/N): N                                          │
 │R10│                                                                    │
 │R11│  Draft or Correspondence quality (D/C): D                          │
 │R12│                                                                    │
 │R13│  Page heading:                                                     │
 │R14│                                                                    │
 │R15│  Esc to cancel                              ↵ to continue          │
 │R16│                                                                    │
 │R17│Profit        │  6,504.68│10,714.54│ 9,969.24│11,947.79│ 39,136.25│ │
 │R18│              │          │VCR INCOME/EXPENSE STATEMENT │            │
 └──────────────────────────────────────────────────────────────────────┘
```

Fig. 6-15. The Print Options Menu to print formulas.

```
                    QTR 1       QTR 2       QTR 3       QTR 4      Year Total

INCOME
  Credit        11,456.77   13,232.00   13,233.50   14,323.44     52,245.71
  Cash           7,645.88    9,811.38   10,220.00   11,767.00     39,444.26
  Other            454.22      555.88      397.00      441.56      1,848.66

Total Income    19,556.87   23,599.26   23,850.50   26,532.00     93,538.63

EXPENSES
  Credit Fees      475.21      527.40      528.60      623.77      2,154.98
  Payroll        2,899.00    2,899.00    2,899.00    3,100.00     11,797.00
  Overhead       8,213.88    7,657.80    8,650.00    8,978.44     33,520.12
  Product Cost     709.11      909.77      870.00      987.00      3,475.88
  Miscellaneous    754.99      890.75      933.66      875.00      3,454.40

Total Expense   13,052.19   12,884.72   13,881.26   14,584.21     54,402.38

Profit           6,504.68   10,714.54    9,969.24   11,947.79     39,136.25
                          VCR INCOME/EXPENSE STATEMENT


                                Page 1
```

Fig. 6-16. The printed spreadsheet.

		C1 QTR 1		C2 QTR 2
R1	INCOME			
		Name: Formula:		Name: Formula:
R2	Credit	11,456.77		13,232.00
		Name: Formula:		Name: Formula:
R3	Cash	7,645.88		9,811.38
		Name: Formula:		Name: Formula:
R4	Other	454.22		555.88
		Name: Formula:		Name: Formula:
R5				
		Name: Formula:		Name: Formula:
R6	Total Income	19,556.87		23,599.26
		Name: Formula: Total(r2c1..r4c1)		Name: Formula: @Total (R2C2..R4C2)

Fig. 6-17. The first page of the formula printout.

```
            Spreadsheet Listing For VCR Example
CELL                CONTENTS

C1 Header           QTR 1
C2 Header           QTR 2
C3 Header           QTR 3
C4 Header           QTR 4

R1 Header           INCOME
R2 Header            Credit
R3 Header            Cash
R4 Header            Other
R6 Header           Total Income
R8 Header           EXPENSES
R9 Header            Credit Fees
R10 Header           Payroll
R11 Header           Overhead
R12 Header           Product Cost
R13 Header           Miscellaneous
R15 Header           Total Expenses
R17 Header           Profit

R2C1                11456.77
R2C2                13232.00
R2C3                13233.50
R2C4                14323.44
R2C5                52245.71

R3C1                 7645.88
R3C2                 9811.38
R3C3                10220.00
R3C4                11767.00
R3C5                39444.26

R4C1                 454.22
R4C2                 555.88
R4C3                 397.00
R4C4                 441.56
R4C5                1848.66

R6C1                           @Total(r2c1..r4c1)
R6C2                           @Total(r2c2..r4c2)
R6C3                           @Total(r2c3..r4c3)
```

Fig. 6-18. The complete spreadsheet with formulas.

R6C4		@Total(r2c4..r4c4)
R6C5		@Total(r2c5..r4c5)
R9C1	475.21	
R9C2	527.40	
R9C3	528.60	
R9C4	623.60	
R9C5	2154.98	
R10C1	2899.00	
R10C2	2899.00	
R10C3	2899.00	
R10C4	3100.00	
R10C5	11797.00	
R11C1	8213.88	
R11C2	7657.80	
R11C3	8650.00	
R11C4	8998.44	
R11C5	33520.12	
R12C1	709.11	
R12C2	909.77	
R12C3	870.00	
R12C4	987.00	
R12C5	3475.88	
R13C1	754.99	
R13C2	890.75	
R13C3	933.66	
R13C4	875.00	
R13C5	3454.40	
R15C1		@Total(R9C1..R13C1)
R15C2		@Total(R9C2..R13C2)
R15C3		@Total(R9C3..R13C3)
R15C4		@Total(R9C4..R13C4)
R15C5		@Total(R9C5..R13C5)
R17C1		R6C1-R15C1
R17C2		R6C2-R15C2
R17C3		R6C3-R15C3
R17C4		R6C4-R15C4
R17C5		R6C5-R15C5
R18C2		VCR INCOME/EXPENSE STATEMENT

PRINTING A SPREADSHEET

To print a spreadsheet at any stage in the creation of one, press the F4 (Print) key as shown in Fig. 6-14. The print menu box tells you that you can print the whole spreadsheet, or just a few selected cells. Press 1, **Print this spreadsheet**. The Print Options Menu appears as shown in Fig. 6-15.

This menu is very similar to the menu to print out documents and files. In this case, however, you can print out the spreadsheet or the formulas. If you answer "no" to the question of printing out the formulas and press the Return or Enter key, the program will ask you to insert a new piece of paper. After you press the Return or Enter key, the spreadsheet will be printed on the paper as shown in Fig. 6-16. In this figure the menu, rows, and columns are not printed. Only the resulting spreadsheet is printed.

If you answer "yes" to the question in the Print Options Menu to print out formulas, all the cells with their formulas, if any, will be printed. Figure 6-17 shows the first of six pages that are printed out. Each cell of the spreadsheet is printed along with its current value or formula, if any. The complete spreadsheet with all the formulas is shown in Fig. 6-18.

If you would like to see a copy of the spreadsheet written to the screen, type **SCREEN** after the "Print to" question. If you would like the spreadsheet printed to a file, type the name of a file after the "Print to" question. This is very useful if you would like the spreadsheet to be inserted in a word processing document.

Chapter 7

Advanced Spreadsheets

This chapter demonstrates some advanced techniques in constructing spreadsheets, including the use of keywords, financial formulas, lookup tables, and if-then-else statements. You also learn how to insert a spreadsheet in a word processing document by the use of setting and finding bookmarks.

KEYWORDS

In Chapter 5 you looked at several keywords, or "built-in" formulas. Most programming languages and spreadsheets have these built-in formulas so that you can just use them instead of writing routines to calculate them. Figure 7-1 shows a spreadsheet that utilizes the keywords of First Choice.

This example shows some computations on five hypothetical test scores which are labeled Test#1, Test#2, etc. You are using the keywords or reserved words of First Choice to do calculations on these five numbers. Figure 7-2 shows a list of the cells with their contents so that you will be able to type them in.

Keyword formulas are entered when you press the ALT F keys at a particular cell. For example, if the cursor is pointing to cell R4C8, you type in the formula ASIN(R3C8). This formula finds an angle whose sine equals 0.50 (the contents of R3C8). Inside the parentheses may be a value, a single or range of cells, or an equation.

As you can see by looking at Fig. 7-1 and Fig. 7-2, you can find the trigonometric function of any number. All the angles that you define are measured in radian measurement and not degrees.

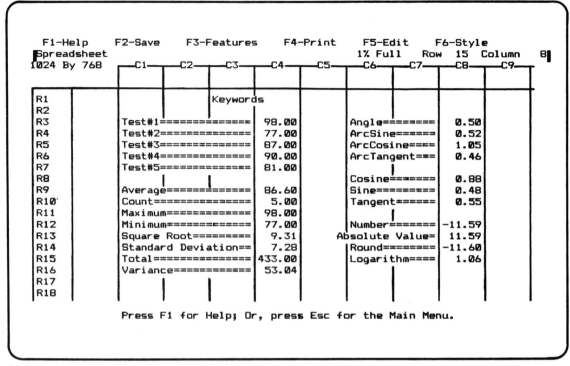

Fig. 7-1. An example of the use of keywords.

The formula in cell R15C8, LOG(R13C8), computes the logarithm of the number 11.59 to the base 10. If the program cannot compute the logarithm of the number, it will print a row of asterisks.

The formula to compute the average is shown in Fig. 7-2 in cell R9C4 as:

Average(R3C4..R7C4)

This formula, or equation, computes the average of all numbers in the cells: R3C4, R4C4, R5C5, R6C6, and R6C7. If any of these cells were left blank, those particular cells would not be included in the average. If any cell had a zero in it, it would be included in the average. For example, the average of the numbers 66, 77, 88, 99 and a cell that had a blank would be 82.5. The average of the numbers 0, 66, 77, 88, and 99 would be 66. Be sure that you understand the difference between the two of them.

The formula could also have been written as follows:

@Average(R3C4..R7C4)

The @ symbol is optional in writing the formula. It may be used with any keyword.

The formula for the average has a range of cells while the trigonometric functions above act only on one cell. Notice that some keywords are typed in uppercase while others are typed in lowercase or some combination of uppercase or lowercase. The value, that is, the result of the formula or expression, is placed in the particular cell the formula is in.

The formula in cell R10C4, Count(R3C4..R7C4), counts how many values are in the cells R3C4, R4C4, R5C4, R6C4, and R7C5. It only counts cells that include numbers, including zero. It will not count any cells that are blank or contain text.

The formula in cell R11C4 is shown below:

Max(R3C4..R7C4) *or* Maximum(R3C4..R7C4)

It finds the largest value in the group of cells. It can be written two ways, as shown above.

The formula shown in cell R12C7 can be written as:

Minimum(R3C4..R7C4) *or* Min(R3C4..R7C4)

It finds the smallest value in the group or range of cells. It can also be written two ways, as shown above.

The formula shown in cell R13C4, SQRT(R9C4), calculates the square root of the value found in cell R9C4. In this case, it finds the square root of 86.60, which is 9.31.

The formula shown in cell R14C4 can be written as:

STDEV(R3C4..R7C4) *or* STD(R3C4..R7C4)

It computes the standard deviation of the values in the cells from R3C4 to R7C4.

The formula shown in cell R16C4 can be written as:

Variance(R3C4..R7C4) *or* Var(R3C4..R7C4)

It computes the variance of the values in the cells from R3C4 to R7C4. The formula shown in cell R15C4 is:

TOTAL(R3C4..R7C4) *or* TOT(R3C4..R7C4)

It sums up the values in the cells from R3C4 to R7C4. The formula shown in cell R13C8, ABS(R12C8), computes the absolute value of −11.59 which is 11.59.

The last formula, shown in cell R14C8 is:

ROUND(R12C8) TO 1

It rounds the number −11.59 to one decimal place so that it becomes −11.6. The word "TO" in the expression followed by the number of decimal places is optional. If you do not use it, the program will assume that you mean to round off to zero decimal places, which will give you an integer.

```
             Spreadsheet Listing Demonstrating Keywords


     CELL              CONTENTS

     R1C3              Keyword
     R1C4              s

     R3C1              Test#1=
     R3C2              =======
     R3C3              =======
     R3C4              98
     R3C6              Angle==
     R3C7              ======

     R4C1              Test#2=
     R4C2              =======
     R4C3              =======
     R4C4              77
     R4C6              ArcSine
     R4C7              ======
     R4C8                            ASIN(R3C8)

     R5C1              Test#3=
     R5C2              =======
     R5C3              =======
     R5C4              87
     R5C6              ArcCosi
     R5C7              ne====
     R5C8                            ACOS(R3C8)
     R6C1              Test#4=
     R6C2              =======
     R6C3              =======
     R6C4              90
     R6C6              ArcTang
     R6C7              ent===
     R6C8                            ATAN(R3C8)

     R7C1              Test#5=
     R7C2              =======
     R7C3              =======
     R7C4              81

     R8C6              Cosine=
```

Fig. 7-2. A spreadsheet listing that demonstrates keywords.

R8C7	======	
R8C8		COS(R3C8)
R9C1	Average	
R9C2	=======	
R9C3	=======	
R9C4		Average(R3C4..R7C4)
R9C6	Sine===	
R9C7	======	
R9C8		Sin(R3C8)
R10C1	Count==	
R10C2	=======	
R10C3	=======	
R10C4		Count(R3C4..R7C4)
R10C6	Tangent	
R10C7	======	
R10C8		TAN(R3C8)
R11C1	Maximum	
R11C2	=======	
R11C3	=======	
R11C4		Max(R3C4..R7C4)
R12C1	Minimum	
R12C2	=======	
R12C3	=======	
R12C4		Minimum(R3C4..R7C4)
R12C6	Number=	
R12C7	======	
R13C1	Square	
R13C2	Root===	
R13C3	=======	
R13C4		SQRT(R9C4)
R13C5	Ab	
R13C6	solute	
R13C7	Value==	ABS(R12C8)
R14C1	Standar	
R14C2	d Devia	
R14C3	tion==	
R14C4		STDEV(R3C4..R7C4)
R14C6	Round==	

```
R14C7                  =======
R14C8                                   ROUND(R12C8) TO 1

R15C1                  Total==
R15C2                  ========
R15C3                  ======
R15C4                                   TOTAL(R3C4..R7C4)
R15C6                  Logarit
R15C7                  hn====
R15C8                                   LOG(R13C8)

R16C1                  Varianc
R16C2                  e======
R16C3                  ======
R16C4                                   Variance(R3C4..R7C4)
```

Fig. 7-2. Continued from page 103.

FINANCIAL FORMULAS

Besides creating your own formulas and using keywords in a spreadsheet, First Choice has several financial formulas that are already built-in. Let's use a formula to see how much interest and principal you are paying on a specific month of a mortgage loan. Figure 7-3 shows a spreadsheet that will accomplish this.

Suppose you have taken out a mortgage loan of $50,000 at 11½% interest for 15 years. The formula will show how much interest and principal you are paying for the 150th payment.

Amount is the name of the variable in cell R1C4. A cell can have a cell name, a coordinate, or both. To see the cell name, move the cursor to R1C4 and press the ALT F keys. The formula box at the bottom right of Fig. 7-3 shows that cell R1C4 is called Amount.

Names can be up to 13 characters in length and must be unique; that is, no two cells can have the same name. They may be typed in uppercase or lowercase letters. Try to name a cell by what it contains. The use of a single letter is valid, but it will not tell you what type of information is in it. If you are trying to type in the name of the cell in the formula box, press the up arrow and the cursor will move to the name field.

In a similar manner, cell R2C4 has the name Rate. Cell R3C4 has the name Number, cell R4C4 has the name Year, and cell R5C4 has the name Period. The complete spreadsheet listing for the mortgage payment formula is shown in Fig. 7-4. After you type in the spreadsheet, you can verify the names by placing the cursor at each of those coordinates and pressing the ALT F keys. If the cell has a name, it will be displayed in the formula box.

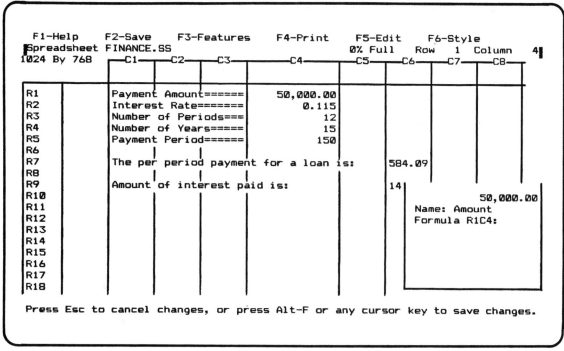

Fig. 7-3. The financial formula for mortgage payments.

The formula to accomplish the pay period for a loan is shown in the formula box of Fig. 7-5. The formula for cell R7C6 is as follows:

PAYMENT ON (Amount) AT (Rate/Number) OVER (Year∗Number)

This formula gives the payment per period for a loan. The amount it prints, $584.09, is the monthly mortgage payment for the life of the loan. The cell Number tells how to compute the interest, which in this case is monthly.

You can see the advantage of naming cells instead of using their coordinates. It is easier to tell what a formula does by looking at the cell name than by trying to figure out what each coordinate represents. An enormous amount of time can be saved in debugging the spreadsheet and trying to correct the errors.

Cell R9C6 also has a built-in financial formula that First Choice understands, as shown in the function box of Fig. 7-6. This formula calculates how much of the monthly payment is interest. In this case, it calculates the amount of interest for the 150th payment. Figure 7-7 shows that the monthly interest for the 150th month is $149.51.

Figure 7-8 shows the built-in formula for the NPV, or net present value. The net present value is used to determine if a project is worth undertaking. This is determined by whether the present value of a project's future cash flow is greater than the initial cost of the project. If this is so, the project is worth undertaking. If the present value is less than the initial cost, the project should be rejected because the investor would lose money if the project were accepted.

Mortgage Payment Spreadsheet

CELL	CONTENTS	
R1C1	Payment	
R1C2	Amount	
R1C3	======	
R1C4	50000	Amount
R2C1	Interes	
R2C2	t Rate=	
R2C3	======	
R2C4	0.115	Rate
R3C1	Number	
R3C2	of Peri	
R3C3	ods===	
R3C4	12	Number
R4C1	Number	
R4C2	of Year	
R4C3	s=====	
R4C4	15	Year
R5C1	Payment	
R5C2	Period	
R5C3	======	
R5C4	150	Period
R6C1	The per	
R6C2	period	
R6C3	paymen	
R6C4	t for a lo	
R6C5	an is:	
R6C6		PAYMENT ON (Amount) AT (Rate/Number) OVER (Year*Number)
R9C1	Amount	
R9C2	of inte	
R9C3	rest pa	
R9C4	id is:	
R9C6		INTEREST ON (AMOUNT) AT (RATE/Number) OVER (Year*NUMBER) FOR (Period)

Fig. 7-4. The spreadsheet listing for mortgage payments.

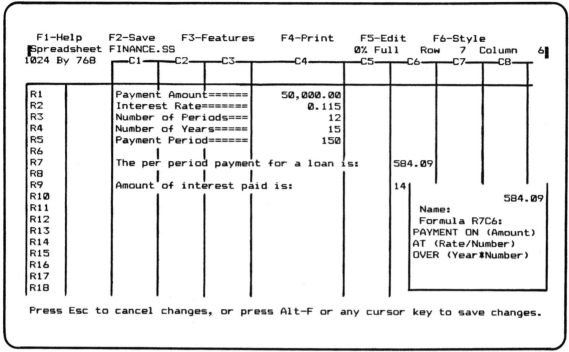

Fig. 7-5. The formula for the pay period on a loan.

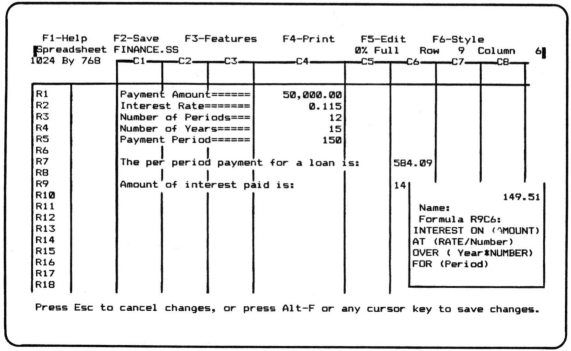

Fig. 7-6. The formula to compute interest payments.

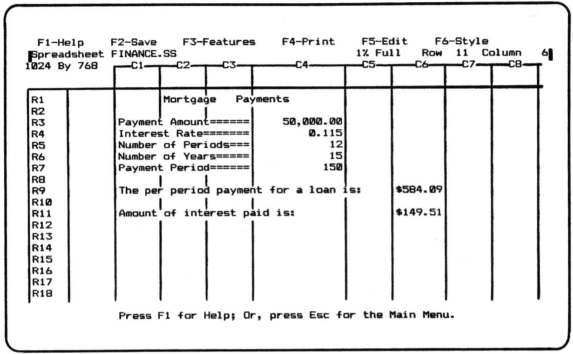

Fig. 7-7. A spreadsheet showing the complete mortgage payment.

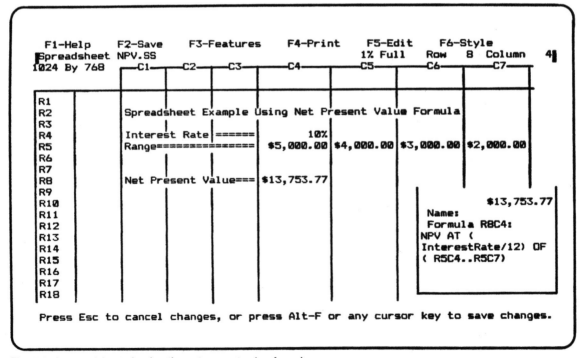

Fig. 7-8. A spreadsheet showing the net present value formula.

The net present value (NPV) of a project can be calculated by the following formula:

NPV = PV − I

PV stands for the present value and I is the initial outlay.

Consider the problem posed in Fig. 7-8. A company is considering an investment that will provide annual after-tax cash flows of $5000, $4000, $3000, and $2000 for five years. If the discount rate of the project is 10% and the initial investment is $10,000, is the project recommended?

The formula for the net present value is:

NPV AT (InterestRate/12) OF (R5C4..R5C7)

The value of InterestRate is shown in cell R4C4 to be ten percent. The range of values that provide after-tax cash flows are in the range of cells R5C4 to R5C7. The present value that is computed by the program is $13,753.77. This means that if the initial investment is $10,000, the net present value is $3,753.77 ($13,753.77 minus $10,000). Because this is a positive number, the project is recommended by the company.

Another financial formula that First Choice provides is one to compute the future value of an investment. An *investment*, or commitment of cash, must provide an increase in value over time. You decide how much money you wish to commit. Then you can calculate how much that money will increase in the future once the expected rate of interest is known. The formula that calculates this is called the *future value of an investment*. Figure 7-9 shows a worksheet that computes the future value of an investment.

Suppose you want to invest $100 every month for three years at a 10% interest rate, compounded monthly. How much money will you have at the end of the three years? The formula to compute the future value, as shown in the formula box of Fig. 7-9, is:

FV ON(AMOUNT) AT (RATE/12) OVER (PERIODS*12)

The reason you are multiplying and dividing by 12 is because you are computing the interest monthly. The interest in all the financial keywords is computed on a period basis. If the interest was calculated per quarter, you would multiply and divide by four. If the interest was calculated weekly, you would multiply and divide by 52.

The future value formula can be used to calculate *annuities*. An annuity is a series of equal payments made in regular intervals of time. They can be made yearly, semiannually, quarterly, or monthly.

The formula reads in the value of AMOUNT from cell R3C4, which in this case is $100. The value of RATE is in cell R4C4, which is 10%. The value of PERIODS, 3, is found in cell R5C4. The final result computed by the formula is shown in cell R7C5. It is $4,178.18. This means that if you invest $100 every

110   Advanced Spreadsheets

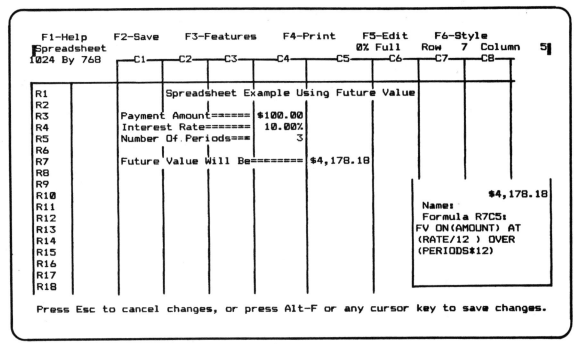

```
  F1-Help      F2-Save      F3-Features     F4-Print      F5-Edit      F6-Style
 Spreadsheet                                            0% Full      Row    7  Column    5
 1024 By 768      —C1——   —C2——  —C3——    —C4——    —C5——   —C6——    —C7——  —C8——

 R1                      Spreadsheet Example Using Future Value
 R2
 R3              Payment Amount======  $100.00
 R4              Interest Rate======   10.00%
 R5              Number Of. Periods===        3
 R6
 R7              Future Value Will Be=========  $4,178.18
 R8
 R9
 R10                                                                            $4,178.18
 R11                                                             Name:
 R12                                                             Formula R7C5:
 R13                                                            FV ON(AMOUNT) AT
 R14                                                            (RATE/12 ) OVER
 R15                                                            (PERIODS*12)
 R16
 R17
 R18

     Press Esc to cancel changes, or press Alt-F or any cursor key to save changes.
```

Fig. 7-9. A spreadsheet showing the future value formula.

month for three years at a 10% interest rate compounded monthly, you will
have $4,178.18.

Another financial formula that is contained in this program is the present
value formula. Figure 7-10 shows a spreadsheet that calculates present value.
It shows how you would calculate the present value of a $100 annuity for a three-
year period. It is assumed that the discount rate is 10%, compounded annually.
The present value formula, shown in the formula box of Fig. 7-10, is the following:

PV ON (AMOUNT) AT (Rate) Over (Periods)

The value of AMOUNT is shown in cell R3C4 as $100.00. The value of
Rate is 10% shown in cell R4C4. The value of Periods is shown in cell R5C4
as 3. The present value is shown in cell R7C4, It is $248.69.

This shows that the three payments of $100 are currently worth only
$248.69. The difference between $300 and $248.69 is called the *total discount*.

To learn about these financial formulas, or *keywords*, as First Choice calls
them, try experimenting by changing any of the values in the cells. Change the
principal, the interest rate, etc. You can see the simplicity and power of
spreadsheets by changing the contents of the various cells.

INSERTING ROWS

Compare Figs. 7-6 and 7-7 and notice the differences. A title followed by
a blank line has been inserted in the heading of Fig. 7-7 to make it more

understandable. To insert a title in Fig. 7-6, place the cursor on the coordinate R1C1 and press the F5 (Edit) key. Press 6, Insert row/column. First Choice will now reply with the following:

Insert row or column(R/C):
Number of rows or columns to insert:

Because you want to insert two rows, type R for row in answer to the first question and 2 for the number of rows. Two rows will be inserted, and you can type in the heading Mortgage Payments.

If you look at Fig. 7-7, you notice that the dollar symbol ($) is printed in columns R9C6 and R11C6. To have the dollar sign printed, press the F6 (Style) key. Press 1, Set cell style, and answer Y to Show currency symbol:. The dollar sign will automatically be inserted for the cell the cursor is positioned over. Do this for both cells, R9C6 and R11C6.

You can try adding another row at the end of the spreadsheet by calculating how much principal is being paid each month. All you have to do is subtract the interest from the monthly payment.

The spreadsheet is now printed by pressing the F4 (Print) key followed by pressing 1, Print this spreadsheet, as shown in Fig. 7-11. When you print the formulas of the spreadsheet, the two financial formulas are printed as shown in Fig. 7-12. This is the fourth page of four pages that are printed.

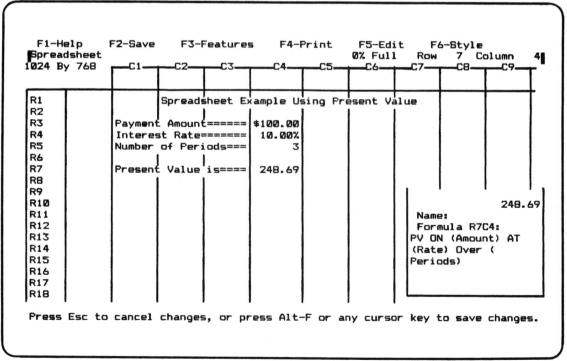

Fig. 7-10. A spreadsheet showing the present value formula.

```
          Mortgage    Payments

Payment Amount======  50,000.00
Interest Rate=======      0.115
Number of Periods===         12
Number of Years=====         15
Payment Period======        150

The per period payment for a loan is: $584.09

Amount of interest paid is:           $149.51
```

Fig. 7-11. An example of printing output of mortgage payments.

LOOKUP TABLES

Values in the spreadsheet can be entered by typing them in or they can be looked up in a table. Postage rates, commission rates, and tax rates are several examples that might be entered in a lookup table. Looking up the weight of a package and finding the corresponding postage rate would save a lot of time and calculations.

Figure 7-13 shows a spreadsheet that has a lookup table. The information in the two cells, R4C3, commission rate, and R5C3, bonus, will be looked up in the table in the bottom of the figure.

Figure 7-14 shows the formula box that demonstrates how the lookup formula works. This cell, R4C3, has both a name, Rate, and a formula. To find the rate, the formula says to look up the value of sales (the name in R3C3) in the table which is located from R13C1 to R18C2. These two coordinates define the limits of the table. It also says to look one column across in the table to find the lookup value.

If you typed in the value $3,000.00, it would search for that value in the table until it found it. It would go across the table one column and find the corresponding rate and place the answer in coordinate R4C3. In this case, it places 0.06 in that particular cell. If you typed in $3,987 or $3,999 it would still give the same commission rate of 0.06. If you typed in $5,000, $5,999, or $6,999, it would give you a commission rate of 0.06. It always gives you the rate corresponding to the sales rounded down to the lowest value in the table. For example, any sales between $5,000 and $7,000 (not including $7,000) would have a commission rate of 0.06. Any sales of $7,000 or over would give you a commission rate of 0.07.

In a similar manner, there is a lookup table for Bonus as shown in Fig. 7-15. This cell, R5C3, has both a name, Bonus, and a formula as shown in the formula box. The formula says to look up the value of sales, and, when sales is found,

```
              150
Name: Period          Name:                    Name:
Formula:              Formula:                 Formula:




Name:                 Name:                    Name:
Formula:              Formula:                 Formula:




t for a lo            an is:                              $584.09
Name:                 Name:                    Name:
Formula:              Formula:                 Formula:
                                               PAYMENT ON (Amount)
                                               AT (Rate/Number)
                                               OVER (Year*Number)




Name:                 Name:                    Name:
Formula:              Formula:                 Formula:




id is:                                                    $149.51
Name:                 Name:                    Name:
Formula:              Formula:                 Formula:
                                               INTEREST ON (AMOUNT)
                                               AT (RATE/Number)
                                               OVER ( Year*NUMBER)
                                               FOR (Period)
```

Fig. 7-12. A printout showing financial formulas.

114 Advanced Spreadsheets

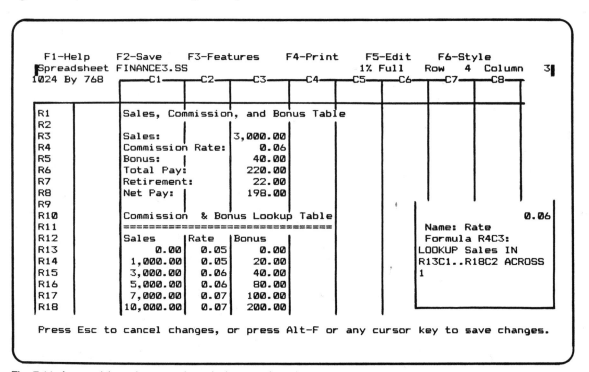

```
   F1-Help     F2-Save    F3-Features     F4-Print     F5-Edit     F6-Style
  Spreadsheet FINANCE3.SS                            1% Full   Row   1  Column   3
  1024 By 768      ─C1──────C2──────C3──────C4──────C5─────C6─────C7──────C8──

 R1              Sales, Commission, and Bonus Table
 R2
 R3              Sales:          3,000.00
 R4              Commission Rate:    0.06
 R5              Bonus:             40.00
 R6              Total Pay:        220.00
 R7              Retirement:        22.00
 R8              Net Pay:          198.00
 R9
 R10             Commission  & Bonus Lookup Table
 R11             ================================
 R12             Sales     │Rate  │Bonus
 R13                 0.00   0.05      0.00
 R14             1,000.00   0.05     20.00
 R15             3,000.00   0.06     40.00
 R16             5,000.00   0.06     80.00
 R17             7,000.00   0.07    100.00
 R18            10,000.00   0.07    200.00

             Press F1 for Help; Or, press Esc for the Main Menu.
```

Fig. 7-13. A spreadsheet demonstrating a lookup table.

```
   F1-Help     F2-Save    F3-Features     F4-Print     F5-Edit     F6-Style
  Spreadsheet FINANCE3.SS                            1% Full   Row   4  Column   3
  1024 By 768      ─C1──────C2──────C3──────C4──────C5─────C6─────C7──────C8──

 R1              Sales, Commission, and Bonus Table
 R2
 R3              Sales:          3,000.00
 R4              Commission Rate:    0.06
 R5              Bonus:             40.00
 R6              Total Pay:        220.00
 R7              Retirement:        22.00
 R8              Net Pay:          198.00
 R9
 R10             Commission  & Bonus Lookup Table                        0.06
 R11             ================================         Name: Rate
 R12             Sales     │Rate  │Bonus                  Formula R4C3:
 R13                 0.00   0.05      0.00                LOOKUP Sales IN
 R14             1,000.00   0.05     20.00                R13C1..R18C2 ACROSS
 R15             3,000.00   0.06     40.00                1
 R16             5,000.00   0.06     80.00
 R17             7,000.00   0.07    100.00
 R18            10,000.00   0.07    200.00

       Press Esc to cancel changes, or press Alt-F or any cursor key to save changes.
```

Fig. 7-14. A spreadsheet demonstrating a lookup rate formula.

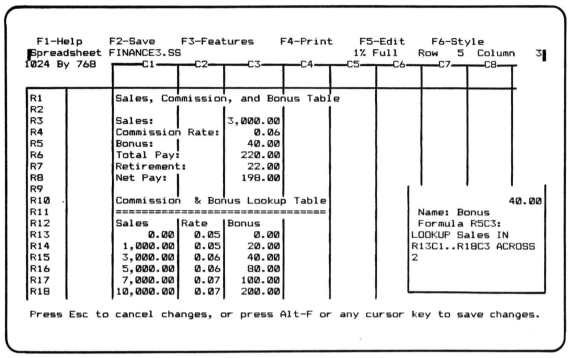

Fig. 7-15. A spreadsheet demonstrating a lookup sales formula.

to go across two columns in the table. The table is located in the coordinates from R13C1 to R18C3 which define the limits of the lookup table.

The formula looks up the value of sales in the first column. In this case, it finds it exactly and goes across two columns to the right to find the corresponding bonus, which is 40.00. Any sales of $3,001, $4,500, or $4,999 would get a bonus of $40.00. Any sales of $5,000, $6,000, or $6,999 would get a bonus of $80.00.

As you can see, lookup tables are very useful for looking up commission rates, sales tax, postage rates, etc. If the rates change, all you have to do is change the values in the table. A lookup table makes the spreadsheet more efficient and less liable to error. If the rates were scattered throughout the spreadsheet, they would be difficult to locate.

The field name TotalPay in cell R6C3 has a name and also a formula as shown in Fig. 7-16. The formula could have been written R2C3*R4C3 + R6C3 instead of Sales*Rate + Bonus. By using field names instead of coordinates, you can see how it makes the formula more understandable and easier to correct if there is an error.

IF-THEN-ELSE STATEMENTS

Besides lookup tables, you can also place IF statements in a formula. The *IF function* allows you to check for certain conditions and then take actions on the results of the check. Suppose, in your hypothetical store, that you and your

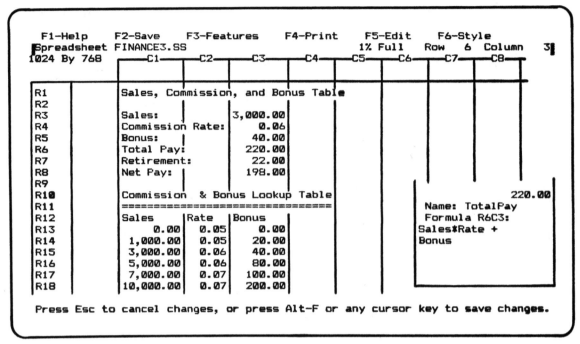

Fig. 7-16. A spreadsheet showing the total pay formula.

employees have decided that if their total pay is $200 or more, then 10% of their total pay would be deducted and placed in a retirement fund. Figure 7-17 illustrates the use of an IF statement.

The formula in the box could have been written as follows:

If TotalPay< =200 Then 0 Else TotalPay*0.10

This formula says that if the total pay is less than or equal to $200, then the value 0 will be placed in the retirement column. If the total pay is greater than $200, then the program will go to the statement following the word Else. It will multiply the total pay by 10% and place the result in the column Retire.

As mentioned in the First Choice manual, you can use the relational operators:

- less than (<)
- greater than (>)
- equal to (=)
- less than or equal to (< =)
- greater than or equal to (> =)
- not equal to (< >)

You can also use the words AND, OR, and NOT. An example of each of them is shown in Fig. 7-18.

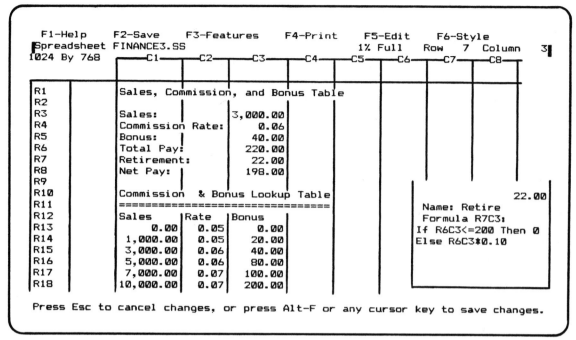

Fig. 7-17. A spreadsheet showing an if-then-else formula.

	IF-THEN-ELSE Statements	
Operator	**Meaning**	**Example**
=	equal to	If Sales = 3,000 then Tax = 0.05
<	less than	If Sales < 3,000 then Tax = 0.04
>	greater than	If Sales > 3,000 then Tax = 0.06
> =	greater than or equal to	If Sales > = 3,000 then Tax = 0.06
< =	less than or equal to	If Sales < = 3,000 then Tax = 0.05
< >	not equal to	If Sales < > 0 then Tax = 0.03 .
AND	two conditions must be true	If (Sales > $3,000) AND (Bonus > $50) then Tax = 0.05
OR	one condition must be true	If (Sales > $3,000) OR (Bonus > $50) then Tax = 0.03
NOT	negates condition	If NOT (Sales > $3,000) then Tax = 0.05 else Tax = 0.03
		(MEANING: If sales is greater than $3,000 then tax is 0.03. If sales is less than or equal to $3,000, the tax is 0.05.)

NOTE: Parentheses are not required but are very useful in understanding the statements.

Fig. 7-18. An example of the use of if-then-else statements.

Using the lookup tables and the IF-Then-Statements in the formulas of the spreadsheets, you can do some sophisticated programming in the cells of the spreadsheet.

SETTING BOOKMARKS

In a previous chapter, you learned how to perform a mail-merge, where information from a file is merged with a word processing document. You also looked at how to combine documents together at print time by using the JOIN command. Spreadsheets can also be merged into other documents through the use of the MERGE command.

To save a spreadsheet to disk, all you have to do is give the spreadsheet a name in the Print Options Menu. For example, Fig. 7-19 shows how to print the spreadsheet FINANCE.SS to a disk file called FINPRT.

This file, after it is saved, will appear on your data disk and will be listed in the Other column. Once this spreadsheet is written to a file name, it can later be inserted into a word processing document by the use of the **Merge another document or spreadsheet** command from the Save Menu. However, there is another way to do this that is easier and faster. First Choice calls it the *bookmark method*.

Suppose you would like to insert the spreadsheet FINANCE.SS into the word processing document LETTER.DOC. Bookmarks enable you to jump around from one document, file, or spreadsheet to another document, file, or spreadsheet. You CANNOT use them with reports. They are used only during

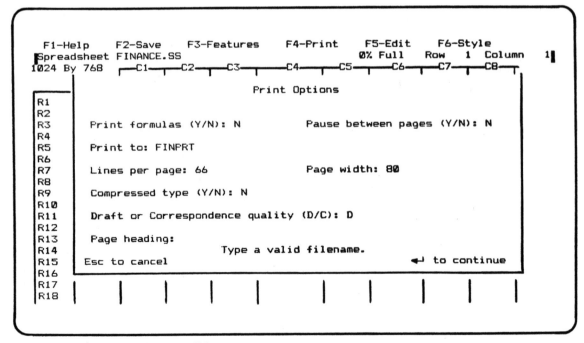

Fig. 7-19. Saving a spreadsheet to a disk.

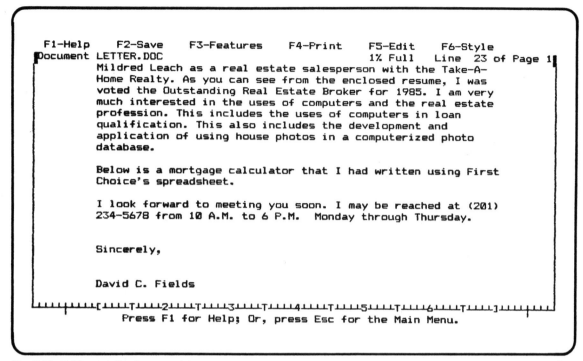

Fig. 7-20. Editing a letter for spreadsheet insertion.

the current session and are not saved. There may be up to six bookmarks per session.

To set the first bookmark, you must first access the word processing document. Access the word processing document LETTER.DOC by pressing 5, **Get an existing file**, from the Main Menu. Insert the three added lines that are shown in Fig. 7-20, starting at line 20. This includes a blank line that is in line 22.

You are going to place one marker in the word processing document and another marker in the spreadsheet. Then you are going to copy the spreadsheet to the clipboard, return to the word processing document, and paste the spreadsheet from the clipboard to the document. It sounds difficult, but it is fairly easy if you use bookmarks.

Place the cursor on column 1 of line 23. It is at this position that you wish to insert a copy of the spreadsheet called FINANCE.SS into your document. You would like to place a marker (bookmark) in this position so that you can go back to it quickly. To set the first bookmark, press the F3 (Features) key and the Features Menu will appear as shown in Fig. 7-21.

Press the 5 key, **Set Bookmark**, and the program will now ask:

Set which bookmark:

Type 1 followed by pressing the Enter or Return key.

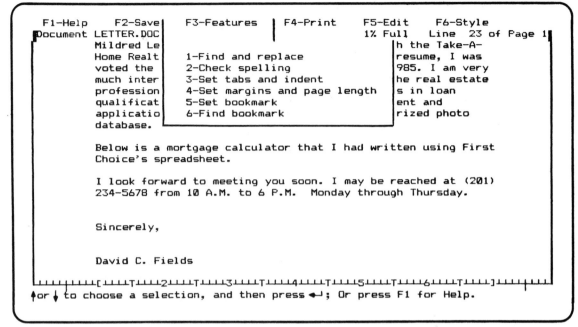

Fig. 7-21. Setting a bookmark.

You would now like to set the second bookmark in the spreadsheet. Exit the LETTER.DOC by pressing the ESC key and return to the Main Menu. Press 5, **Get an existing file,** and retrieve the spreadsheet FINANCE.SS. Set another marker by placing the cursor in row 1, column 1. Press the F3 (Features) key. Press 5, **Set Bookmark,** and the program will again ask:

Set which bookmark:

Type 2 followed by pressing the Enter or Return key.

FINDING BOOKMARKS

Now that the bookmarks are set, you would like to insert the spreadsheet into the word processing document. If you are not in it already, access the word processing document LETTER.DOC. Place the cursor on column 1, line 23. This is where you would like to insert the spreadsheet. Press the F3 (Features) key followed by pressing 6, **Find Bookmark.** Figure 7-22 appears, showing the two bookmarks that you set previously.

Each bookmark gives the type and name of the file used in the bookmark, along with the page, line, and column number. As you can see, you can set up to six bookmarks in one session. Press 2 to access the spreadsheet FI-NANCE.SS.

You should now be in column 1, row 1 of the file FINANCE.SS. This is the spreadsheet that you would like to insert in the word processing document.

```
 F1-Help    F2-Save    F3-Features    F4-Print    F5-Edit    F6-Style
Document BOOKMK.DOC                              1% Full   Line  23 of Page 1
          voted the Outstanding Real Estate Broker for 1985. I am very

          Find which bookmark:
             1 — Document 'BOOKMK.DOC', page 1, Line 23.
             2 — Spreadsheet 'FINANCE.SS', Row 1, Column 1.
             3 — Not used.
             4 — Not used.
             5 — Not used.
             6 — Not used.



          Esc to cancel                         ↵  to continue


          David C. Fields

└┴┴┴┴┴┤┴┴┴┴┴[┴┴┴┴T┴┴┴2┴┴┴┴T┴┴┴3┴┴┴┴T┴┴┴4┴┴┴┴T┴┴┴5┴┴┴┴T┴┴┴6┴┴┴┴T┴┴┴]┴┴┴┴┴┤┴┴┴┴┴
```

Fig. 7-22. Finding a bookmark.

```
 F1-Help    F2-Save    F3-Features    F4-Print    F5-Edit    F6-Style
Document LETTER.DOC                              2% Full   Line  15 of Page 1
          profession. This includes the uses of computers in loan
          qualification. This also includes the development and
          application of using house photos in a computerized photo
          database.

          Below is a mortgage calculator that I had written using First
          Choice's spreadsheet.

                 Mortgage   Payments

          Payment Amount====== 50,000.00
          Interest Rate=======    0.115
          Number of Periods===       12
          Number of Years=====×      15
          Payment Period======      150

          The per period payment for a loan is: $584.09

          Amount of interest paid is:          $149.51

          I look forward to meeting you soon. I may be reached at (201)
└┴┴┴┴┴┤┴┴┴┴┴[┴┴┴┴T┴┴┴2┴┴┴┴T┴┴┴3┴┴┴┴T┴┴┴4┴┴┴┴T┴┴┴5┴┴┴┴T┴┴┴6┴┴┴┴T┴┴┴]┴┴┴┴┴┤┴┴┴┴┴
          Press F1 for Help; Or, press Esc for the Main Menu.
```

Fig. 7-23. Inserting a spreadsheet in a document.

KEYWORDS AND FINANCIAL FUNCTIONS

Command	Explanation
ABS(X)	Computes the absolute value of X.
ACOS(X)	Computes the angle whose cosine equals X in radians, where X is between −1 and 1.
ASIN(X)	Computes the angle whose sine equals X in radians, where X is between −1 and 1.
ATAN(X)	Computes the angle in radians whose tangent equals X.
AVG(X)	Computes the average of all values in the range.
COS(X)	Computes the cosine of X, where X is an angle in radians.
COUNT(X)	Counts the number of cells that have numeric data in them.
FV ON(Payment amount) AT(interest rate) OVER(number of periods)	Computes the future value of a series of equal payments at a certain rate over a period of time. For example, FV ON(100) AT(10%/12) OVER(3∗12) = $4,178.18. You are dividing and multiplying by 12 to give you the monthly interest rate.

IF(conditional equation) THEN(value) ELSE(value)

Operator	Meaning
=	equal to
<	is less than
>	is greater than
< =	is less than or equal to
> =	is greater than or equal to
< >	is not equal to
AND	two conditions must be true to get the value after the THEN
OR	one condition must be true to get the value after the THEN
NOT	negates the condition

For example, IF SALES > 1000 Then TAX = .1 Else TAX = .05
If the values of sales is over $1000, the tax is 10%, otherwise the tax is 5%.

Command	Explanation
INTEREST ON(amount) AT(interest rate) OVER(number of periods) FOR(payment period)	Calculates the amount of interest you will have paid in a series of payments at a given interest rate on a loan. For example: INTEREST ON(50000) AT(.115/12) OVER(15∗12) FOR(12) = $149.51 This gives the amount of interest during the twelfth monthly payment on a $50,000 15-year loan at an interest rate of 11.5%.
LOOKUP(value) IN(range) ACROSS(number of columns)	Looks up a value in a range of cells and places the result in a cell.

Fig. 7-24. Keyword and financial functions.

Command	Explanation

		C1	C2	C3
	R12	Sales	Rate	Bonus
	R13	0	0.05	0
	R14	1000	0.06	20
	R15	3000	0.07	40
	R16	5000	0.08	60

If you type in the keyword expression: LOOKUP 4567 IN (R13C1 . . R16C1) ACROSS 2 the value of 40 will be placed in the cell. The number 4567 is between R15C1 and R16C1. It rounds down to 3000 and goes two across to find the Bonus value of 40.

MAX(*range*)
MAXIMUM(*range*)

Finds the largest value in a range of cells.

MIN(*range*)
MINIMUM(*range*)

Finds the smallest value in a range of cells.

NPV AT(*interest rate*)
OF(*range*)

Finds the Net Present Value of a series of future cash flows. The interest rate is the cost of money that is used to discount the future cash flows or the discount rate. The range is a series of cells found in one column or row that contain the amount of cash payments after the initial cash outlay. For example, NPV AT(10%/12) OF(R5C4 . . R5C7) gives the current cash value of the payments in Row 5, Columns 4 through 7, when discounted at a 10% annual rate.

PAYMENT ON(*amount*)
AT(*interest rate*)
OVER(*number of periods*)

Computes the payment you need to make on a loan over a given time period at a specific interest rate. For example, PAYMENT ON($50,000) AT(.115/12) OVER(15∗12) = $584.09 computes the mortgage payment on a $50,000 loan at 11.5% annual interest for a period of 15 years which is $584.09.

PV ON(*amount*) **AT**(*rate*)
OVER(*number of periods*)

Computes the present value of a series of equal payments at a specific interest rate over a specified period of time. For example, PV ON($100) AT(10%) OVER 3 = $248.69 gives you the present value of a series of three $100 payments at 10% interest is $248.69.

ROUND(*X*) **TO** (*Y*)

Rounds the value of X to Y decimal places. If you want to round off to the nearest integer, set Y to 0 or leave off the number following the TO.

SIN(*X*)

Computes the sine of X, where X is measured in radians.

STDEV(*range*)
STD(*range*)

Computes the standard deviation of the values in the range.

TAN(*X*)

Computes the tangent of X, where X is measured in radians.

TOTAL(*range*)
TOT(*X*)

Calculates the sum of the values in the range.

VAR(*range*)
VARIANCE(*range*)

Computes the variance of all values in the range.

You must now copy it to the clipboard so it can later be pasted into the word processing document. Press the F5 (Edit) key followed by pressing 1, **Select Cells**. Press the Tab key five times, then press the down arrow key 11 times. The whole spreadsheet should now be highlighted.

Press the F5 (Edit) key followed by pressing 3, **Copy selected cells to clipboard**. Now that the spreadsheet is in the clipboard, press the F3 (Features) key followed by pressing 7, **Find bookmark**. You would like to jump back to the word processing document and paste the spreadsheet. The program asks you:

Find which bookmark:

Type 1 followed by pressing the Return or Enter key.

To insert the spreadsheet in the document, press the F5 (Edit) key followed by pressing 5, **Paste from clipboard**. The spreadsheet is now inserted in the word processing document as shown in Fig. 7-23.

The bookmark method is very useful if you have to jump from one document to another. It avoids using the Main Menu so it saves a lot of time. It is especially useful if you want to copy and paste one document into another.

SUMMARY

Figure 7-24 gives a summary of the mathematical and statistical functions that can be used with the spreadsheets discussed in this chapter.

Chapter 8

Communications

This chapter defines what data communications is and how to use the communications module of First Choice to access a service, another computer, or dial a telephone number in a file.

BACKGROUND

Writing reports at home or in a business can be very frustrating. It seems that you are always missing pieces of information that are located at a library, office, or friend's home. The problem is that you do not have the time to get to it.

Communications software—software that electronically links a personal computer to another computer system—provides a way to quickly and accurately communicate with distant sources of information. These software packages can be linked to a friend's personal computer so that messages, programs, and data can be exchanged. A personal computer is easily linked to a larger computer system so that data and programs stored on the larger computer can be transferred, or *downloaded*, to the personal computer.

Your microcomputer is capable of communications as well as information processing. Your microcomputer can link with a telephone system to send and receive data to and from virtually anywhere in the world. To implement this capability, your microcomputer must be equipped with a modem and a communications program.

A *modem* is a special hardware device that acts as a link between a microcomputer and a telephone system. It enables you to connect with a communications service or another computer. The sending and receiving machines must be compatible to handle identical signals. Establishing a connection is a relatively easy task with the help of the communications module from First Choice.

Your microcomputer can now enter the world of information-related services. Some examples of these services involve obtaining stock quotations, using banking services, obtaining airline and restaurant reservations, using news services, using consumer buying services, and software exchange.

ELECTRONIC MAIL

Electronic mailboxes are spaces within computer-maintained files for receiving messages that are assigned to users. Messages addressed to specific users can be sent directly to the appropriate mailboxes. These messages are received automatically. Users can check their mailboxes for messages on a regular basis.

Many large organizations use electronic mail techniques for their personnel. The telephone has limitations because you must find the right person at the right time. Much time is lost trying to get two people on the line simultaneously. In most situations, it is a case of one person talking to an answering machine. A letter between these two people might solve the problem, but a letter might take several days to reach its destination. Electronic mail provides a solution to these problems. It provides the speed of the telephone and the guaranteed message delivery of the postal system.

Another advantage of electronic mail is that messages may be sent to one or more specific mailboxes. The owner of your VCR shop might send one message to a top salesperson, or another to several salespersons to inform them of a meeting that is to take place. Messages are addressed to certain recipients through codes embedded within a message file. The person who receives these messages can save them to disk or transfer to a printer or other output device.

There are many forms of electronic mail services. Many subscription services are offered by commercial carriers such as MCI, The Source, CompuServe, Western Union, ITT, etc. Some of these are discussed later in this chapter. Many of these services, such as The Source and CompuServe, provide bulletin boards and information services.

BULLETIN BOARDS

An electronic bulletin board can be thought of as a large mailbox shared by several users. Messages posted to bulletin boards are shared by any user accessing the board.

Bulletin boards are often set up for special-interest groups or organizations. There are user groups for specific makes of microcomputers that often exchange hints, upgrade tips, and other information over bulletin boards. One example of a special interest group would be one set up for people who collect coins. Wants lists and buy lists can be exchanged with conditions and prices.

Some bulletin boards are set up with electronic mailboxes available for private message exchanges. In the coin example, a bid on a certain coin can be sent to one specific mailbox or person.

Bulletin boards can also be an excellent source for free or inexpensive software. Many bulletin boards provide collections of *public domain* software. This software can be copied by any user. These programs are written by individuals and made available to any user who accesses the bulletin board. The originators of the software might ask for minimal and/or voluntary payments from users. Almost any application that is covered by a commercial package can also be found in some type of public domain software.

Bulletin boards are set up and maintained on some type of computer. Depending upon the size of the board, and the number of users, microcomputers might provide enough capacities to handle incoming calls and messages. Once the computer is set up, most of the work is performed by the computer without human intervention. Some bulletin boards give a telephone number that can be used for personal help to handle questions about the program.

Some bulletin boards are too large to run on microcomputers. However, all of them are designed to be accessed by microcomputers.

NETWORKING

Within some organizations or databases, microcomputers can be linked in arrangements known as *networks* to share data and information. Microcomputer terminals may be linked to minicomputers or mainframes. Under this arrangement, users are provided access to many or all of the resources maintained by the larger machines. These networks make use of uploading and downloading.

Uploading refers to capabilities for sending data from remote terminals to the minicomputer or mainframe, using remote terminals to manipulate data maintained on larger machines. *Downloading* is the reverse of this process. Files or processing capabilities are transferred from the central computer to microcomputer terminals. Data communications techniques provide virtually limitless opportunities for sharing data resources.

INFORMATION SERVICES

Information service organizations maintain files for public access and provide special services to callers. Subscribers pay fees for the services they use. Information services provide information on virtually any subject: personal finance, entertainment, education, health, business, etc. Below is a description of three of the more popular information services that are found in the First Choice Service Menu.

COMPUSERVE

CompuServe is based in Columbus, Ohio and is the country's largest information service, with over 200,000 subscribers. It was bought by H&R Block in 1980 and is available 24 hours a day from anywhere in the world.

CompuServe is used both by the consumer and the businessperson through its Consumer Information Service and Executive Information Service. The CompuServe Information Service carries stories and features from newspapers, wire services, and organizational profiles; financial news; electronic banking and fund transfer; airline scheduling and reservation services; movie, theater, book, and restaurant reviews; medical and health information; electronic games; mail service and shopping; on-line encyclopedias; personal computing software; and many other features and software.

CompuServe Information Service's CB lets you carry on a conversation on its channels so that it appears that your computer is acting like a regular citizens band radio. You can assume a handle or name so that nobody else will know who you are. Enter **GO CB** at CompuServe's Main Menu and you are ready to go.

In CompuServe, there are many groups devoted to IBM standard personal computers. To enter where the IBM games are located, type **GO IBMNEW** from the Main Menu of CompuServe. Here you'll find games, personal opinions, and free utility programs.

The Comp-U-Store is the electronic mail-order catalog of CompuServe where you can order any merchandise, from clothing and travel to food and liquor. Anything you order will arrive by UPS or Federal Express. Most of the prices are higher than local stores, but it eliminates the time spent shopping and travelling. As you buy things, CompuServe charges your credit card or withdraws money directly from your bank account. Don't go wild with this one or you'll wind up in the poor house!

A subscriber to the Executive Information Service has access to all the options just discussed. In addition, he or she can have access to a range of financial, demographic, and editorial information. Stock quotes and commodity prices are available. Historical market information, market and industry indexes, and national and international news wire services are also available.

A subscriber using CompuServe can do research for a presentation, make airline reservations to a distant city where the presentation will be given, transfer funds among bank accounts to pay for the flight, send messages to arrange for an airport pickup, check reviews of restaurants in that city, and even consult weather reports to help pack the appropriate clothing for the trip. This can all be done with a single communication.

THE SOURCE

The Source is based in McLean, Virginia and was founded as an information network by Source Telecomputing Corporation in 1979. It was later acquired by The Reader's Digest Association, Inc., in 1980. Its transmissions are carried by Telenet and other networks, allowing members to reach The Source with a local telephone call.

The Source is mainly business-oriented. It had about 62,000 subscribers in mid-1985. Over half the subscribers that use The Source use it for business purposes.

The Source provides many of the same types of information as CompuServe, such as news stories, electronic mail, classified ads, financial information, entertainment reviews, and financial services.

DOW JONES NEWS

The Dow Jones News Retrieval Service provides business and financial services to users. These services include stock market quotations, profiles of business organizations, financial news, and financial forecasts, as well as general news and information. The Dow Jones News Retrieval was started in 1974 to offer financial news to stockbrokers via ticker tape. In 1979, the financial service was opened up to anyone who had access to a personal computer. Quotations on stocks can easily be accessed any time of the day. Dow Jones News also carries the text *The Wall Street Journal* and other well known financial publications.

A MODEM

The information services are available for a minimal investment. All that is needed is a microcomputer equipped with a modem and a telephone. Once this hardware is installed, establishing communications is a matter of travelling through the menu structure of the communications module and the services themselves.

In order to communicate with another computer, your personal computer has to be physically connected to the telephone line. This requires a hardware interface called a modem. On the transmitting end, a modem converts the *binary signals* (ones and zeros) produced by a computer or peripheral device to *analog signals*, which can be sent over the public telephone system. On the receiving end, the modem converts the analog signal back to a digital signal which is forwarded to the computer or associated device.

Data in its most basic form is a series of electronic pulses in two varieties. These values are represented numerically as *bits* (binary digits), zero and one. Every character (for example, a letter or a number) consists of eight bits, or one *byte*, according to the commonly accepted ASCII coding scheme. *ASCII* is an abbreviation for American Standard Code for Information Exchange. For example, the letter A is represented by the code 01000001, the number 9 by the code 00111001, and the quotation symbol (") is represented by the code 01010110.

Every message transmitted by a computer, whether it is a word, number, or even a picture, is broken down into bytes. These bytes are further broken down into bits. A computer processes information one byte at a time, while a telephone line carries a message one bit at a time. A device known as a *serial port* is needed to convert the parallel stream of eight bits to a serial stream for transmission, then back again on the receiving end.

Another problem is that the telephone was built for voice transmission. The telephone is an analog device that represents information in a continuous, smoothly varying signal. A computer is a digital device that uses discrete signals, representing data as the presence or absence of an electrical voltage.

Modem is an abbreviation for modulator and demodulator. A *modulator* converts a digital signal to an analog one. A *demodulator* does the reverse; it converts an analog signal to a digital signal. A modem is a device that performs both functions, connecting personal computers to the telephone system.

Chapter 1 of this book mentions that you must use the Set Up Menu of First Choice if you have a modem that is not Hayes-compatible. Choosing a modem is the first step in beginning telecommunications. Just as with every other kind of PC peripheral, there are many modems commercially available, which differ in price and capability. The speed of a modem, the maximum rate at which it can transmit or receive data, is one of the more important distinguishing characteristics. This rate is measured in bits per second (bps) or *baud*. In most cases, the two terms are used interchangeably.

Three hundred bps is considered low speed for a data transfer rate. Medium speed is 1200 to 9600 bps. Anything over 9600 is high speed. Most high-speed modems require specifically installed data communication lines and are not suitable for personal computers.

In general, as the rate of a modem increases so does the price, but the cost of all modems is dropping. A few years ago, 300 bps was the standard transfer rate for most personal computers. Now 1200 bps is becoming the standard, while the 2400 bps rate will be the standard over the next few years.

Even though the high-speed modems cost more, they return some savings in the form of reduced communications costs. Most information services such as CompuServe and The Source charge according to the amount of "connect time." Therefore, the faster the modem, the less time it takes to transmit data, resulting in lower communications costs. It takes approximately one minute to fill a 24-by-80 screen at 300 baud. On the other hand, it only takes 16 seconds to fill the screen at the 1200 baud rate and eight seconds at the 2400 baud rate.

Modems are also chosen according to their physical design. Some can fit into an expansion slot inside the personal computer's system while others can stand alone on a desk-top. An internal modem is generally cheaper than an external modem. It does not require additional desk space because it is contained entirely within the system unit. It also does not require an outside, or extra, power supply.

External modems work with a variety of personal computers. This is useful when you expect to change from one make of computer to another, as from IBM to Apple. It is also easier to set switches and control volume on external modems. They also have flashing lights on the front of the unit to help you monitor the status of the telephone call. An external modem takes up additional desk space and requires its own electrical outlet.

One type of external modem is an *acoustic coupler*. An acoustic coupler plugs into a computer and connects to a standard telephone. The handset of the telephone is inserted into a pair of rubber cups. Carrier signals are produced and received through the mouthpiece and earpiece of the telephone handset.

```
                    Service Menu


          1-CompuServe
          2-Dialog Business Con.
          3-Dow Jones News
          4-MCI Mail
          5-Official Airline Gd.
          6-The Source
          7-Other service
          8-Other service
          9-Answer incoming call
```

↑ or ↓ to choose a selection, and then press ↵;

Or press F1 for Help.

Fig. 8-1. The Service Menu.

When you choose the Set Up Equipment Menu, you may indicate which modem you have. First Choice assumes that you have a touch-tone telephone system. If you have a rotary system, you must also change that setting.

After the modem setting has been saved, you can then access the communications module by pressing 6, **Connect to another computer**, from the Main Menu. The Service Menu now appears as shown in Fig. 8-1.

CHOOSING A SERVICE

To choose a service, all you have to do is type in that particular number. If your service is not listed in the menu, you may save it by typing it in at 7 or 8, **Other service**. Suppose that you wish to access CompuServe. Press the 1 (CompuServe) key and the service information screen for CompuServe appears as shown in Fig. 8-2.

Press the Tab key once to move the cursor to the telephone number field. You must now type in the telephone number for CompuServe. The number can include parentheses, spaces, or hyphens. To answer the rest of the questions, you must check the manual that comes with your particular modem.

If you wish to create an *automatic sign-on*, answer Y to the third question in the service information. When you have finished entering all the information, press the Return or Enter key to save the information.

```
                        Service Information


     Service name: CompuServe
     Phone number:
     Create automatic sign-on (Y/N): N

     Communication speed: 300
     Data bits (7 or 8): 8
     Stop bits (1 or 2): 1
     Parity (none,even,odd,mark,space): NONE
     Full or half duplex (F/H): F
     Use XON/XOFF (Y/N): Y


     Esc to cancel                      ↵ to continue
```

Fig. 8-2. Service Information.

If you use the automatic sign-on, every time you access the CompuServe Service Menu, the telephone number will be dialed when you press the F10 key. If you wish to stop an automatic sign-on at any time, press the ESC key.

When you log on to a service, the on-line screen appears. First Choice will always give you the *communications status*, letting you know if you are connected to another computer or not. It will also tell you how much of your computer's CPU (central processing unit) is taken up by the computer transmission.

Check the communications speed for the speed of your modem. It might be 300 baud, 1200 baud, 2400 baud, or some other speed.

The next question asks you for the number of *data bits*. The default for using ASCII characters is seven bits. Type in eight bits if you are using non-ASCII formats, including extended character sets or binary data that uses all eight bits.

The next question asks you for the number of *stop bits*. The default value is one. The bits in a message travel in groups. Data is sent and received one character at a time. Stop bits are added to identify the end of a data character transmission. One or two stop bits may be added to the end of each character.

The question on parity must be answered by checking your modem manual. All data communications are subject to *noise*, or disturbances on the line. This can alter the value of the transmitted data and produce garbled messages. Parity checking is a technique designed to detect these types of errors. A parity bit is an extra bit that is added to every byte. It is used to check whether the bits in a byte have been altered in transmission. Parity normally is specified as odd or even.

The value of the parity bit depends on the other bits in the byte. If the parity is specified as even, then in each byte the total number of bits that are ones, including the parity bit, must be even. For example, the letter T is represented by the ASCII code 01010100. A parity bit representing a one is added at the end of the byte to make it an even parity. It now becomes 010101001. There are now four ones in the code, making it even parity. If there is already an even number of ones in the code, a zero parity bit is added. For example, the letter U in ASCII code is represented by 01010101. When the parity bit is added, it becomes 010101010. The parity bit is set to 0 because there is already an even number of ones.

The next question asks you if you are using half or full duplex. Communications channels are characterized as *half duplex* or *full duplex* depending on the direction of data flow. Full duplex permits data to flow in both directions simultaneously, while half duplex permits data to flow in only one direction at a time.

Half-duplex transmission is analogous to a two-way street undergoing construction. Traffic is halted at one end of the street and allowed to pass in one direction. Traffic is then halted at the other end of the street and permitted to pass in the opposite direction. Half-duplex transmission requires devices that can both send and receive. The half-duplex line can be shifted from one direction of data flow to the other, but its utility is still limited. If a terminal is transmitting data over a half-duplex circuit, the computer cannot interrupt the input flow to send back an important message. It must wait until the terminal shifts the circuit to the receive mode before delivering the information.

A full-duplex channel transmits data in both directions simultaneously. It is analogous to a two-way street with traffic passing in both directions. Each end of a full-duplex line is assigned to a different frequency so that messages don't interfere with one another. Transmission of data is faster than with half-duplex. This is because the system is not burdened with overhead created by continuously reversing direction.

A full-duplex transmission is the most efficient. Suppose an operation is entering data through a terminal to the computer and is unaware that the system's storage capacity has reached its limit. With a full-duplex circuit, the computer can signal the terminal to stop inputting data before the system becomes overloaded. Full-duplex transmission is the mode used most often by personal computers.

Finally, First Choice asks you if you wish to use the XON/XOFF. The default is Yes. This is a form of *protocol*, or *handshaking*, used when two devices initially establish communications with one another. The communications settings are stored in a file so that reestablishing the connection, if disconnected, is much easier.

When information is received in your computer, it is received as a word processing document. You can also send a word processing document, a spreadsheet, a report, or a group of records. This is accomplished by pressing the F3 (Features) key. The First Choice manual will tell you how to send, transmit, receive, and exchange files. To disconnect the modem, press the F3

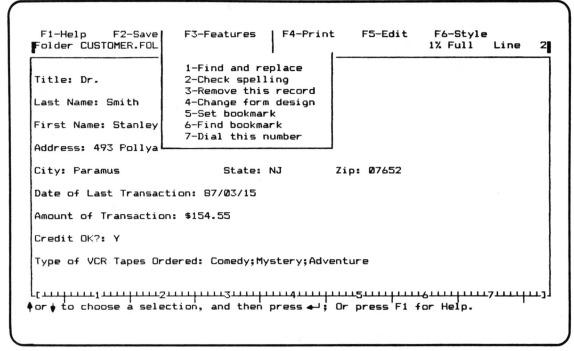

Fig. 8-3. Dialing a telephone number.

(Features) key followed by pressing the 5 (Disconnect) key. Once you are disconnected from the service or another computer, you can edit the document, print the document, or save it to your disk.

DIALING A NUMBER FROM A RECORD

Besides dialing services and talking to other computers, First Choice will let you dial a telephone number that is listed in a record. Figure 8-3 shows a record in the Customer file. To have the program dial a number, you need a modem and a field that has a telephone number in it. Place the cursor on the phone number of the record that you wish to have dialed. Press the F3 (Features) key followed by pressing 7, Dial this number, as shown in Fig. 8-3. The number will automatically be dialed.

STOPPING AND STARTING TRANSMISSION

In most cases, you can stop transmission by pressing the CTRL S keys. You can restart transmission by pressing the CTRL Q keys. Some information services require you to use special keys to start and stop transmission. Be sure to look at the Help screen of those services.

Appendices

Appendix A

Spreadsheet Business Applications

You can use the spreadsheet module of First Choice for recording checks and deposits for a one month period. You can design this register so that it is useful for both business and personal applications.

CHECK REGISTER

Suppose you plan to record the following information: the check number, the date, a description of the check, the amount of the check, the amount of the balance, and a running balance. Figure A-1 shows a printout of the check register.

If you want to add some more rows to accommodate additional checks or deposits, just use the insert a row/column command in the Edit Menu. You can create a separate spreadsheet for each month of the year or you can combine several months together. Figure A-2 gives a list of all the values and formulas in the cells.

ALTERNATIVE INVESTMENTS USING NPV

There is a stream of uneven cash flow in most investment examples. To choose the best project from several alternatives, you must discount the projected cash flow to the present. You can then select the project or projects with the highest present value. As mentioned in Chapter 7, First Choice has a built-in function to compute the net present value. This example utilizes that formula.

```
   F1-Help      F2-Save     F3-Features     F4-Print     F5-Edit     F6-Style
  Spreadsheet                                            1% Full   Row  15  Column   6
  1024 By 768    ─C1──  ──C2──  ──C3──  ──C4──  ──C5──  ──C6──  ──C7──  ──C8──

 R1           │Check Register  │       │       │Jan.    │1988   │
 R2  ======  ===========================================================================
 R3  NUMBER│DATE│DESCRIPTION  │  │CHECK   │DEPOSIT│        │BALANCE
 R4           │BALANCE FORWARD           │          │        │$2,000.00
 R5  100    │Park Realty  │  │$750.00 │        │$1,250.00
 R6  101    │Paper Supply │  │ $55.00 │        │$1,195.00
 R7  102    │Electric Co. │  │$227.00 │        │  $968.00
 R8  700    │Deposit      │  │        │$550.00 │$1,518.00
 R9  103    │Telephone Co.│  │$235.00 │        │$1,283.00
 R10 104    │Gas Co.      │  │ $88.00 │        │$1,195.00
 R11 701    │Deposit      │  │        │$128.00 │$1,067.00
 R12
 R13
 R14 ======  ===========================================================================
 R15        │   │TOTALS│  │$1,355.00│$678.00│
 R16
 R17
 R18

          Press F1 for Help; Or, press Esc for the Main Menu.
```

Fig. A-1. The check register.

In your example, you are considering two investments. The projected cash flow for each investment is as follows:

Year	Investment#1	Investment#2
1988	11000	2000
1989	12000	11000
1990	12000	16000
1991	12000	21000
1992	13000	21000

You wish to calculate the net present values for each cash flow stream. Using the net present value financial function, you can easily analyze alternative investments as shown in Fig. A-3.

You can see what happens if discount rates, down payments, or cash flows are changed. When designing the spreadsheet, place the values that are likely to change in a table. You can then easily locate them to make the appropriate changes.

The format of the report allows the easy extension of the cash flows to any number of periods. The interest rate is positioned so it can easily be changed.

```
CELL            CONTENTS

R1C1            Check Register
R1C6            Jan.
R1C7            1988

R2 Heading      ======
R2C1            ==========================================

R3 Heading      NUMBER
R3C1            DATE
R3C2            DESCRIPTION
R3C5            CHECK
R3C6            DEPOSIT
R3C8            BALANCE

R4C2            BALANCE FORWARD
R4C8            2000

R5 Heading      100
R5C2            Park Realty
R5C6            750
R5C8            R4C8-R5C5

R6 Heading      101
R6C2            Paper Supply
R6C5            55
R6C8            R5C8-R6C5

R7 Heading      102
R7C2            Electric Co.
R7C5            227
R7C8            R6C8-R7C5

R8 Heading      700
R8C2            Deposit
R8C6            550
R8C8            R7C8+R8C6

R9 Heading      103
R9C2            Telephone Co.
R9C5            235
R9C8            R8C8-R9C5

R10 Heading     104
R10C2           Gas Co.
R10C5           88
R10C8           R9C8-R10C5

R11 Heading     701
R11C2           Deposit
R11C6           128
R11C8           R10C8+R11C6

R14 Heading     ======
R14C2           ==========================================

R15C3           TOTALS
R15C5           @TOTAL(R5C5..R11C5)
R15C6           @TOTAL(R5C6..R11C6)
```

Fig. A-2. A spreadsheet listing for the check register.

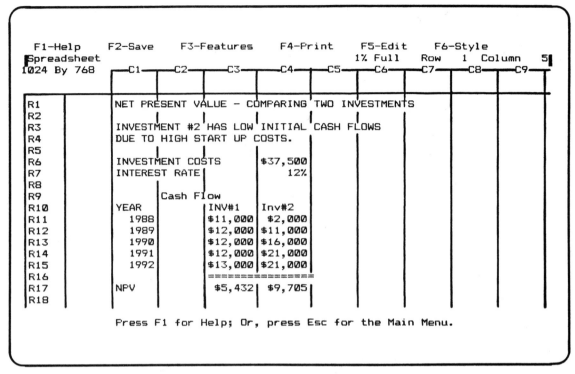

Fig. A-3. Comparing investments with net present value.

As shown in the output, the NPVs are the following:

Investment #1 = $5,432
Investment #2 = $9,705

You would therefore choose Investment #2 because it has the higher NPV. The listing of all the formulas and values is shown in Fig. A-4.

STOCK PORTFOLIO

The First Choice spreadsheet module is a perfect tool for quickly analyzing a stock portfolio. As your portfolio grows, you can easily add the new purchases by adding rows to the model. You can also add columns for additional calculations you want to perform on each stock. All the information that you wish to know about the stocks can be kept in the spreadsheet. Figure A-5 shows a small model stock portfolio.

One change that you can make to the spreadsheet is to list the purchases for the same stock and keep a total average price on file to use in calculating your gains or losses. You can also include the Dow Jones Industrial Average index at the time of purchase and keep a plus (+) or minus (−) figure to reflect the stock's relative performance. Figure A-6 shows a listing of the spreadsheet with all the formulas and values.

CELL	CONTENTS
R1C1	NET PRESENT VALUE - COMPARING TWO INVESTMENTS
R3C1	INVESTMENT #2 HAS LOW INITIAL CASH FLOWS
R4C1	DUE TO HIGH START UP COSTS
R6C1	INVESTMENT COSTS
R6C4	37500
R7C1	INTEREST RATE
R7C4	12%
R9C2	Cash Flow
R10C1	YEAR
R10C3	INV#1
R10C4	INV#2
R11C1	1988
R11C3	11000
R11C4	2000
R12C1	1989
R12C3	12000
R12C4	11000
R13C1	1990
R13C3	12000
R13C4	16000
R14C1	1991
R14C3	12000
R14C4	21000
R15C1	1992
R15C3	13000
R15C4	21000
R16C3	===============
R17C1	NPV
R17C3	-R6C4 + NPV AT (R7C4) OF (R11C3..R15C3
R17C4	-R6C4 + NPV AT (R7C4) OF (R11C4..R15C4)

Fig. A-4. A spreadsheet listing for comparing investments.

```
   F1-Help      F2-Save     F3-Features      F4-Print     F5-Edit    F6-Style
  Spreadsheet STOCK.SS                                     1% Full   Row   3  Column    4
  1024 By 768 ──C1────C2────────C3────────C4────C5───────C6────────C7────┬─C8──┐
 ┌────────────┬───────┬──────────┬───────┬──────┬─────────────┬────────┬────────┐
 │R1          │       │STOCK PORTFOLIO    │      │             │        │        │
 │R2          │NAME OF│NUMBER    │PURCH  │CURR  │GAIN/        │DIV PER │YIELD   │
 │R3          │STOCK  │   OF SHARES│PRICE │PRICE │LOSS         │SHARE   │        │
 │R4          │       │          │       │      │             │        │        │
 │R5          │N Y Tel│1000.00   │$44.50 │$53.00│ $8,500.00   │0.00    │0.00    │
 │R6          │Apple  │1500.00   │$44.50 │$53.13│$12,945.00   │0.30    │0.56    │
 │R7          │IBM    │2000.00   │$79.75 │$76.50│$-6,500.00   │0.88    │1.15    │
 │R8          │McDonalds│1000.00 │$50.00 │$66.13│$16,130.00   │0.99    │1.50    │
 │R9          │       │          │       │      │             │        │        │
 │R10         │       │          │       │      │             │        │        │
 │R11         │TOTALS │5500.00   │       │      │$31,075.00   │        │3.21    │
 │R12         │       │          │       │      │             │        │        │
 │R13         │       │          │       │      │             │        │        │
 │R14         │       │          │       │      │             │        │        │
 │R15         │       │          │       │      │             │        │        │
 │R16         │       │          │       │      │             │        │        │
 │R17         │       │          │       │      │             │        │        │
 │R18         │       │          │       │      │             │        │        │

      Press F1 for Help; Or, press Esc for the Main Menu.
```

Fig. A-5. A stock portfolio.

DEPRECIATION SCHEDULE

In accounting, there are several methods for computing depreciation on equipment. The spreadsheet for this example uses the declining balance method. This provides for large depreciation early in the life of the equipment to calculate annual depreciation. It also shows the cumulative total of depreciation which helps to avoid exceeding the total allowable depreciation.

The example shown in Fig. A-7 shows a computer that costs $5,500, has a life of seven years, and has a salvage value at the end of the period of $850. Therefore, the total depreciation that is allowed is $4,650 ($5,500 − $850). The declining balance is twice straight-line depreciation, which generates a factor of 28.57%. In year 1, $1,571.43 may be claimed. By year 6, $172.64 is all that can be claimed without exceeding total depreciation. Figure A-8 shows a listing of the spreadsheet with all the formulas and values.

BALANCE SHEET

The balance sheet model as shown in Fig. A-9 provides a business balance sheet that details assets, liabilities, and stockholders equity.

If you insert or delete items from any area of this model, be sure to check that total costs balance with total liabilities and stockholders equity. You might want to separate such accounts as bad debt reserve or other assets. Figure A-10 shows a listing of the spreadsheet with all the formulas and values.

CELL	CONTENTS
R1C2	STOCK PORTFOLIO
R2C1	NAME OF
R2C3	NUMBER
R2C4	PURCH
R2C5	CURR
R2C6	GAIN/
R2C7	DIV PER YIELD
R3C1	STOCK
R3C2	OF SHARES
R3C4	PRICE
R3C5	PRICE
R3C6	LOSS
R3C7	SHARE
R5C1	N Y Tel
R5C3	1000
R5C4	44.5
R5C5	53
R5C6	(R5C3*R5C5)-(R5C3*R5C4)
R5C7	0.00
R5C8	R5C7/R5C5*100
R6C1	Apple
R6C3	1500
R6C4	44.5
R6C5	53.13
R6C6	(R6C3*R6C5)-(R6C3*R6C4)
R6C7	0.30
R6C8	R6C7/R6C5*100
R7C1	IBM
R7C3	2000
R7C4	79.75
R7C5	76.5
R7C6	(R7C3*R7C5)-(R7C3*R7C4)
R7C7	0.88
R7C8	R7C7/R7C5*100
R8C1	McDonalds
R8C3	1000
R8C4	50
R8C5	66.13
R8C6	(R8C3*R8C5)-(R8C3*R8C4)
R8C7	0.99
R8C8	R8C7/R8C5*100
R11C1	TOTALS
R11C3	@TOTAL(R5C3..R8C3)
R11C6	@TOTAL(R5C6..R8C6)
R11C8	@TOTAL(R5C8..R8C8)

Fig. A-6. A spreadsheet listing for sample stock portfolio.

```
    F1-Help    F2-Save    F3-Features    F4-Print    F5-Edit    F6-Style
   Spreadsheet DECBAL.SS                            2% Full   Row   1 Column   3
   1024 By 768    C1      C2        C3        C4       C5        C6   C7       C8

  R1                   Depreciation Schedule: Declining Balance
  R2
  R3          ITEM:           Computer         Total Depreciation
  R4          COST:           5,500.00         Allowed:                  4,650.00
  R5          LIFE:               7.00
  R6          SALVAGE VALUE     850.00         Straight Line times           2.00
  R7                                           D/B Factor:                  28.57
  R8
  R9                  Deprec   Cumultv  Max      Amt To
  R10         Year    Calc'd    Total   Allowed  Claim
  R11
  R12             1 1,571.43 1,571.43 4,650.00 1,571.43
  R13             2 1,122.45 2,693.88 3,078.57 1,122.45
  R14             3   801.75 3,495.63 1,956.12   801.75
  R15             4   572.68 4,068.30 1,154.37   572.68
  R16             5   409.06 4,477.36   581.70   409.06
  R17             6   292.18 4,769.54   172.64   172.64
  R18             7   208.70 4,978.25  -119.54  -119.54

             Press F1 for Help; Or, press Esc for the Main Menu.
```

Fig. A-7. A declining balance shown through a depreciation schedule.

TIME SHEET

If you have a business that deals in consulting or some other type of service that is billed by the hour, then you can use a spreadsheet to keep track of the billing amounts as shown in Fig. A-11.

You can keep one spreadsheet per client. All you have to do is enter the time spent each day along with the appropriate rate code. The rate table at the top of the chart can be adjusted any time by just changing the rate in the table. The lookup function finds the rate that corresponds to that particular code and computes the amount. The spreadsheet shown in Fig. A-12 makes use of the lookup function of First Choice.

VALUE OF INVENTORY

This First Choice model calculates an ongoing value of inventory based on a weighted average cost of all items in stock. You provide the unit cost and quantity of each item added to the inventory and the total number of stock items sold since the last report.

The inventory volume carried forward and the weighted average cost from the previous quarter must be supplied from the previous report.

The sample model is based on figures for a store that sells floppy disks for the second quarter of the year. Throughout the quarter, new stock was purchased on various days and at various prices. New stock has a weighted

CELL	CONTENTS
R1C2	Depreciation Schedule: Declining Balance
R3C1	ITEM:
R3C3	Computer
R3C5	Total Depreciation
R4C1	COST:
R4C3	5500
R4C5	Allowed:
R4C8	R4C8-R6C3
R5C1	LIFE:
R5C3	7
R6C1	SALVAGE VALUE
R6C3	850
R6C5	Straight Line times
R6C8	2
R7C5	D/B Factor:
R7C8	100/R5C3*R6C8
R9C2	Deprec
R9C3	Cumultv
R9C4	Max
R9C5	Amt To
R10C1	Year
R10C2	Calc'd
R10C3	Total
R10C4	Allowed
R10C5	Claim
R12C1	1
R12C2	R4C3*R7C8/100
R12C3	R12C2
R12C4	R4C8
R12C5	min(r12c2..r12c4)

Fig. A-8. A spreadsheet listing for a sample stock portfolio.

R13C1	2
R13C2	R4C3*R12C3*(100/7*2/100)
R13C3	R12C3+R13C2
R13C4	R4C8 − R12C3
R13C5	min(r13c2..r13c4)
R14C1	3
R14C2	R4C3*R13C3*(100/7*2/100)
R14C3	R13C3+R14C2
R14C4	R4C8 − R13C3
R14C5	min(r14c2..r14c4)
R15C1	4
R15C2	R4C3*R14C3*(100/7*2/100)
R15C3	R14C3+R15C2
R15C4	R4C8 − R14C3
R15C5	min(r15c2..r15c4)
R16C1	5
R16C2	R4C3*R15C3*(100/7*2/100)
R16C3	R15C3+R16C2
R16C4	R4C8 − R15C3
R16C5	min(r16c2..r16c4)
R17C1	6
R17C2	R4C3*R16C3*(100/7*2/100)
R17C3	R16C3+R17C2
R17C4	R4C8 − R16C3
R17C5	min(r17c2..r17c4)
R18C1	7
R18C2	R4C3*R17C3*(100/7*2/100)
R18C3	R17C3+R18C2
R18C4	R4C8 − R17C3
R18C5	min(r18c2..r18c4)

Fig. A-8. Continued from page 145.

average unit cost of $1.75. Prior to this quarter there were 350 units in stock with an average unit cost of $2.59. Averaging the previous average cost per item and the current average cost per item provides a new weighted average unit costs for the 535 units in stick. On June 30 a current weighted value of $1,160.87 is produced as shown in Fig. A-13. Figure A-14 shows a listing of the spreadsheet with all the formulas and values.

```
                        VCR COMPANY
                       BALANCE SHEET
               YEAR END: December 31, 1988

                          ASSETS
CURRENT ASSETS:
Cash                                           2,320,000
US Government Bonds                              820,000
Accounts Receivable                            2,661,000
Inventories                                    3,231,800
Prepaid Insurance, Taxes, Other Expenses         220,000

        Total Current Assets..............     9,252,800

PROPERTY, PLANT, & EQUIPMENT

Land                                 289,000
Buildings                  3,406,100
Equipment                 12,529,000
                          ============
                          15,935,100
        Less Allowance For
            Depreciation  -8,118,000 7,817,100

    Total Property, Plant, & Equipment.......  8,106,100

    Total Assets............................. 17,358,900


                        LIABILITIES

CURRENT LIABILITIES:

ACCOUNTS PAYABLES                                990,800
ACCRUED PAYROLL, TAXES, INTEREST, ETC.         1,045,000
ESTIMATED INCOME TAXES                           190,700
DUE ON LONG TERM DEBT                            200,000
                                             ===========
        Total Current Liabilities             2,426,500

LONG-TERM DEBT(S)                              2,677,500
OTHER LIABILITIES                                      0
                                             ===========
        Total Liabilities                     5,104,000


                   STOCKHOLDERS' EQUITY

PREFERRED STOCK                     1,126,000
COMMON STOCK                        2,173,000
CONTRIBUTED CAPITAL                 2,085,000
RETAINED EARNINGS                   6,870,900

        Total Stockholders' Equity            12,254,900

        Total Liabilities & Stockholders' Equity  17,358,900



                         Page 1
```

Fig. A-9. A balance sheet.

CELL	CONTENTS
R1C3	VCR COMPANY
R2C3	BALANCE SHEET
R3C3	YEAR END: DECEMBER 31, 1988
R5C3	ASSETS
R6C1	CURRENT ASSETS:
R7C1	Cash
R7C7	2320000
R8C1	US Government Bonds
R8C7	820000
R9C1	Accounts Receivable
R9C7	2661000
R10C1	Inventories
R10C7	3231800
R11C1	Prepaid Insurance, Taxes, Other Expenses
R11C7	220000
R13C2	Total Current Assets....................
R13C7	@TOT(R7C7..R11C7)
R15C1	PROPERTY, PLANT, & EQUIPMENT
R17C1	Land
R17C6	289000
R18C1	Buildings
R18C5	3406100
R19C1	Equipment
R19C5	12529000
R20C5	============
R21C5	R18C5+R19C5
R22C2	Less Allowance For
R23C3	Depreciation
R23C5	-8118000
R23C6	R21C5+R23C5
R25C2	Total Property, Plant, & Equipment.........
R25C7	R17C6+R23C6

Fig. A-10. A spreadsheet listing for the balance sheet.

```
R27C2        Total Assets.............................
R27C7        R13C7+R25C7

R30C3        LIABILITIES

R32C1        CURRENT LIABILITIES:

R34C1        ACCOUNTS PAYABLE
R34C7        990800

R35C1        ACCRUED PAYROLL, TAXES, INTEREST, ETC.
R35C7        1045000

R36C1        ESTIMATED INCOME TAXES
R36C7        190,700

R37C1        DUE ON LONG TERM DEBT
R37C7        200000

R38C7        =========

R39C2        Total Current Liabilities
R39C7        @Total(R34C7..R37C7)

R41C1        LONG-TERM DEBT(S)
R41C7        2677500

R42C1        OTHER LIABILITIES
R42C7        0

R43C7        =========

R44C2        Total Liabilities
R44C7        @TOTAL(R39C7..R42C7)

R47C3        STOCKHOLDERS' EQUITY

R49C1        PREFERRED STOCK
R49C6        1126000

R50C1        COMMON STOCK
R50C6        2173000

R51C1        CONTRIBUTED CAPITAL
R51C6        2085000

R52C1        RETAINED EARNINGS
R52C6        687900

R54C2        Total Stockholders' Equity
R54C7        @TOT(R49C6..R52C6)

R56C2        Total Liabilities & Stockholders' Equity
R56C7        R44C7+R54C7
```

```
   F1-Help     F2-Save     F3-Features     F4-Print     F5-Edit     F6-Style
  Spreadsheet                                          1% Full    Row   1  Column   5
  1024 By 768    C1     C2     C3     C4     C5     C6     C7     C8     C9

 R1              |TIME  |SHEET
 R2             <HOURLY RATE CHART>
 R3
 R4              CODE  |RATE
 R5              ==============
 R6                 1| 25.00
 R7                 2| 35.00
 R8                 3| 50.00
 R9
 R10             DATE  |CODE  |RATE  |HOURS  |AMOUNT
 R11             =======================================
 R12             Jan 5 |    2| 35.00 |  2.0| $70.00
 R13             Jan 8 |    1| 25.00 |  7.5| $187.50
 R14             Jan 9 |    3| 50.00 |  5.0| $250.00
 R15             Jan 10|    2| 35.00 |  4.5| $157.50
 R16             Jan 15|    2| 35.00 |  8.0| $280.00
 R17             =======================================
 R18                   |      |Totals| 27.00| $945.00

        Press F1 for Help; Or, press Esc for the Main Menu.
```

Fig. A-11. A time sheet.

PERSONAL NET WORTH

The spreadsheet model can help you assess your personal net worth. You enter all your assets and liabilities. The model will total the assets and deduct the liabilities. The spreadsheet is shown in two parts for ease of viewing. The asset portion is shown in Fig. A-15.

The liabilities and net worth portion is shown in Fig. A-16. This model is designed to accommodate all categories of assets and liabilities. You can add entries to whatever categories you want to make it more complete. Figure A-17 shows a listing of the spreadsheet with all the formulas and values.

DIRECT-MAIL CAMPAIGN

You can create a spreadsheet model that calculates the cost of a direct mailing. It analyzes the sales and returns generated by the mailing. The way it is set up is for the sale of a single product. Figure A-18 show the printout of the spreadsheet.

The input to the spreadsheet would be the postage rate, the number of pieces that are mailed, and other costs to produce the mailing.

The responses to the mailing are kept in a different portion of the spreadsheet. The input to this part of the spreadsheet would be the number of responses per week and the number of the units sold. The spreadsheet calculates the total returns, percentage of total returns, and cost per sale. Figure A-19 shows a listing of the spreadsheet with all the formulas and values.

CELL	CONTENTS
R1C2	TIME
R1C3	SHEET
R2C1	<HOURLY RATE CHART>
R4C1	DATE
R4C2	CODE
R4C3	RATE
R4C4	HOURS
R4C5	Amount
R5C1	=============
R6C1	1
R6C2	25
R7C1	2
R7C2	35
R8C1	3
R8C2	50
R11C1	===
R12C1	Jan 5
R12C2	2
R12C3	Lookup R12C2 in R6C1..R8C3 Across 1
R12C4	2
R12C5	R12C4*R12C3
R13C1	Jan 8
R13C2	1
R13C3	Lookup R13C2 in R6C1..R8C3 Across 1
R13C4	7.5
R13C5	R13C4*R13C3
R14C1	Jan 9
R14C2	3
R14C3	Lookup R14C2 in R6C1..R8C3 Across 1
R14C4	5
R14C5	R14C4*R14C3

Fig. A-12. A spreadsheet listing for the time sheet.

```
R15C1              Jan 10
R15C2              2
R15C3              Lookup R15C2 in R6C1..R8C3 Across 1
R15C4              4.5
R15C5              R15C4*R15C3
R16C1              Jan 15
R16C2              2
R16C3              Lookup R16C2 in R6C1..R8C3 Across 1
R16C4              8.0
R16C5              R16C4*R16C3

R17C1              ==============================================

R18C3              Totals
R18C4              @TOTAL (R12C4..R16C4)
R18C5              @TOTAL (R12C5..R16C5)
```

Fig. A-12. Continued from page 151.

```
     VALUE OF INVENTORY

SALE OF FLOPPY DISKS          INVENTORY END OF QTR #1
Inventory Carried Forward From Previous Quarter=      350
Weighted Average From Previous Quarter=              2.59

        Purchases
Purchase        Unit   Quantity      Total
Date            Price                Price
Apr 11          2.88    500        1,440.00
Apr 22          1.90    750        1,425.00
May 17          0.99  1,000          990.00
May 15          1.50    875        1,312.50
June 1          2.50    400        1,000.00
June 9          1.75    650        1,137.50
------------------------------------------------
                Total  4,175       7,305.00
                Sold   3,990

Weighted Average Cost This Quarter     1.75

              Inventory on June 30      535

End Of Quarter Weighted Value    1,160.87
```

Fig. A-13. The value of inventory.

CELL	CONTENTS
R1C2	VALUE OF INVENTORY
R3C1	SALE OF FLOPPY DISKS
R3C5	INVENTORY END OF QTR #1
R4C1	Inventory Carried Forward From Previous Quarter=
R4C8	350
R5C1	Weighted Average From Previous Quarter=
R5C8	2.59
R7C2	Purchases
R8C1	Purchase
R8C3	Unit
R8C4	Quantity
R8C6	Total
R9C1	Date
R9C3	Price
R9C6	Price
R10C1	Apr 11
R10C3	2.88
R10C4	500
R10C6	R10C3*R10C4
R11C1	Apr 22
R11C3	1.90
R11C4	750
R11C6	R11C3*R11C4
R12C1	May 17
R12C3	0.99

Fig. A-14. A spreadsheet listing for the value of inventory.

```
R12C4              1000
R12C6              R12C3*R12C4


R13C1              May 15
R13C3              1.50
R13C4              875
R13C6              R13C3*R13C4


R14C1              June 1
R14C3              2.50
R14C4              400
R14C6              R14C3*R14C4


R15C1              June 9
R15C3              1.75
R15C4              650
R15C6              R15C3*R15C4


R16C1              -----------------------------------------------


R17C3              Total
R17C4              @TOTAL(R10C4..R15C4)
R17C6              @TOTAL(R10C6..R15C6)


R18C3              Sold
R18C4              3990


R20C1              Weighted Average Cost This Quarter
R20C6              R17C6/R17C4


R22C3              Inventory on June 30
R22C6              R4C8+R17C4-R18C4


R24C1              End of Quarter Weighted Value
R24C6              (R5C8+R20C6)/2*R22C6
```

Fig. A-14. Continued from page 153.

```
            PERSONAL NET WORTH STATEMENT

            ASSETS
========================================
Current Monetary Assets:
        Cash On Hand             300.00
        Checking Accounts        975.00
        Savings Accounts         450.00
                Sub-Total      1,725.00

Current Market Value of Securities:
        Stocks                   444.00
        Bonds                    567.00
        Mutual Funds             778.00
        Other                      0.00
                Sub-Total      1,789.00

Current Cash Value of
        Long Term Assets:
Certificates of Deposit        6,700.00
US Savings Bonds                 900.00
IRA                            7,500.00
Annuities                      3,760.00
Life Insurance                   823.00
Retirement Plan                8,232.00
                Sub-Total     27,915.00

Current Market Value of
        Durable Assets:
Home, Coop, Condo            175,000.00
Automobiles                    9,675.00
Clothing                       3,450.00
Jewelry                        1,368.00
Antiques                         876.00
Stamps, Coins, Etc.              550.00
Furniture                      4,430.00
                Sub-Total    195,349.00

Total Current Asset Value    226,778.00
```

Fig. A-15. A personal net worth statement—assets.

```
                    LIABILITIES
=============================================
Current Bills Due:
        Charge Cards              2,500.00
        Medical Bills              330.00
        Dental Bills               880.00
        Electric                   288.00
        Gas                         33.00
        Auto Insurance             770.00
        Life Insurance             335.00
        Medical Insurance          244.00
        Tuition                    345.00
                Sub-Total        5,725.00

Loans to be Paid
        Mortgage               125,000.00
        Installment Loan         5,645.00
        Home Improvement         4,000.00
        Life Insurance             500.00
        Education Loans          7,666.00
                Sub-TotTal     142,811.00


Taxes to be Paid
        Real Estate Taxes          900.00
        Federal Income           3,450.00
        State & Local              678.00
        Self Employment          1,209.00
                Sub-ToTal        6,237.00

Total Current Liability Value
        ===================>   154,773.00

New Worth================>      72,005.00
```

Fig. A-16. A personal net worth statement—liabilities.

CELL	CONTENTS
R1C2	PERSONAL NET WORTH STATEMENT
R3C2	ASSETS
R4C1	===
R5C1	Current Monetary Assets:
R6C2	Cash On Hand
R6C5	300
R7C2	Checking Accounts
R7C5	975
R8C2	Savings Accounts
R8C5	450
R9C3	Sub-Total
R9C5	@TOTAL(R6C5..R8C5)
R11C1	Current Market Value of Securities:
R12C2	Stocks
R12C5	444
R13C2	Bonds
R13C5	567
R14C2	Mutual Funds
R14C5	778
R15C2	Other
R15C5	0
R16C3	Sub-Total
R16C5	@TOTAL(R12C5..R12C5)
R18C1	Current Cash Value of

Fig. A-17. A spreadsheet for the personal net worth statement.

R19C2	Long Term Assets
R20C1	Certificates of Deposit
R20C5	6700
R21C1	US Savings Bonds
R21C5	900
R22C1	IRA
R22C5	7500
R23C1	Annuities
R23C5	3760
R24C1	Life Insurance
R24C5	823
R25C1	Retirement Plan
R25C5	8232
R26C3	Sub-Total
R26C5	@Total(R20C5..R25C5)
R28C1	Current Market Value of
R29C2	Durable Assets:
R30C1	Home, Coop, Condo
R30C5	175000
R31C1	Automobiles
R31C5	9675
R32C1	Clothing
R32C5	3450
R33C1	Jewelry
R33C5	1368
R34C1	Antiques
R34C5	876
R35C1	Stamps, Coins, Etc.
R35C5	550

Fig. A-17. Continued from page 157.

```
R36C1              Furniture
R36C5              4430

R37C3              Sub-Total
R37C5              @TOTAL(R30C5..R36C5)

R39C1              Total Current Asset Value
R39C5              R9C5+R26C5+R37C5

R42C2              LIABILITIES

R43C1              ===========================================

R44C1              Current Bills Due:

R45C2              Charge Cards
R45C5              2500


R46C2              Medical Bills
R46C5              330

R47C2              Dental Bills
R47C5              880

R48C2              Electric
R48C5              288

R49C2              Gas
R49C5              33

R50C2              Auto Insurance
R50C5              770

R51C2              Life Insurance
R51C5              335

R52C2              Medical Insurance
R52C5              244

R53C2              Tuition
R53C5              345

R54C3              Sub-Total
R54C5              @Total(R44C5..R53C5)
```

R56C1	Loans to be paid
R57C2	Mortgage
R57C5	125999
R58C2	Installment Loan
R58C5	5645
R59C2	Home Improvement
R59C5	4000
R60C2	Life Insurance
R69C5	500
R61C2	Education Loans
R61C5	7666
R62C3	Sub-Total
R62C5	@TOTAL(R57C5..R61C5)
R65C1	Taxes to be Paid
R66C2	Real Estate Taxes
R66C5	900
R67C2	Federal Income
R67C5	3450
R68C2	State & Local
R68C5	678
R69C2	Self Employment
R69C5	1209
R70C3	Sub-Total
R70C5	@TOTAL(R66C5..R69C5)
R72C1	Total Current Liability Value
R73C2	========================>
R73C5	154773
R75C2	Net Worth================>
R75C5	72005

Fig. A-17. Continued from page 159.

```
           DIRECT MAIL CAMPAIGN

UNIT RETAIL PRICE:        110.00

CURRENT POSTAGE RATE (3rd):    0.0850
NUMBER OF PIECES MAILED:   8,000.00
NET COST OF CAMPAIGN:      4,377.00
RETURN POSTAGE:               37.54
                           ----------
Total Cost of Campaign:    4,414.54

                                      Cost
Leads          % of      Cost    Units  Per   Total
Returned       Mailing   /Lead   Sold   Sale  Sales      Profit
  370            4.63    8.45    75.00  58.86 8,250.00 3,835.46



        Leads               Percent        Percent
                            Of Total       Of Total
Week#   Returns             Mailings       Returns
  1       40                  0.50          10.81
  2       55                  0.69          14.86
  3       50                  0.63          13.51
  4      155                  1.94          41.89
  5       35                  0.44           9.46
  6       25                  0.31           6.76
  7       10                  0.13           2.70
==============              =======================
Total    370                  4.63

        Largest % Returns in One Week=    41.89

COSTS
====================
Paper            85.00
Printing        750.00
Folding          85.00
Typesetting     130.00
Envelopes        18.00
Stuffing         89.00
Postage         680.00
Services      2,500.00
Miscellaneous    40.00
              ---------
      Total   4,377.00
```

Fig. A-18. A direct mail campaign.

CELL	CONTENTS
R1C2	DIRECT MAIL CAMPAIGN
R3C1	UNIT RETAIL PRICE:
R3C4	110
R5C1	CURRENT POSTAGE RATE (3rd):
R5C5	.085
R6C1	NUMBER OF PIECES MAILED:
R6C5	8000
R7C1	NET COST OF CAMPAIGN:
R7C5	4377
R8C1	RETURN POSTAGE:
R8C5	37.54
R9C5	---------
R10C1	Total Cost of Campaign:
R10C5	R7C5+R8C5
R12C7	Cost
R13C1	Leads
R13C3	% of
R13C4	Cost
R13C6	Units
R13C7	Per
R13C8	Total
R14C1	Returned
R14C3	Mailing
R14C4	/Lead
R14C6	Sold
R14C7	Sale
R14C8	Sales
R14C9	Profit
R15C1	370
R15C3	R15C1/R6C5*100
R15C4	R15C1/R7C5*100
R15C6	75
R15C7	R10C5/R15C6
R15C8	R15C6*R3C4
R15C9	R15C8-R10C5

Fig. A-19. A spreadsheet for direct mailing.

```
R20C2          Leads
R20C5          Percent
R20C6          Percent

R21C5          Of Total
R21C6          Of Total

R22C1          Week#
R22C2          Returns
R22C5          Mailings
R22C6          Returns

R23C1          1
R23C2          40
R23C5          R23C2/R6C5*100
R23C6          R23C2/R31C2*100

R24C1          2
R24C2          55
R24C5          R24C2/R6C5*100
R24C6          R24C2/R31C2*100

R25C1          3
R25C2          50
R25C5          R25C2/R6C5*100
R25C6          R25C2/R31C2*100

R26C1          4
R26C2          155
R26C5          R26C2/R6C5*100
R26C6          R26C2/R31C2*10

R27C1          5
R27C2          35
R27C5          R27C2/R6C5*100
R27C6          R27C2/R31C2*10

R28C1          6
R28C2          25
R28C5          R28C2/R6C5*100
R28C6          R28C2/R31C2*10

R29C1          7
R29C2          10
R29C5          R29C2/R6C5*100
R29C6          R29C2/R31C2*10

R30C1          =================

R30C5          ==========================
```

```
        R31C1           Total
        R31C2           @TOT(R23C2..R29C2)
        R31C5           @TOT(R23C5..R29C5)

        R33C4           Largest % Returns in One Week=
        R33C6           @MAX(R23C6..R29C6)

        R35C1           COSTS

        R36C1           ================================

        R37C1           Paper
        R37C3           85

        R38C1           Printing
        R38C3           750

        R39C1           Folding
        R39C3           85

        R40C1           Typesetting
        R40C3           130

        R41C1           Envelopes
        R41C3           18

        R42C1           Stuffing
        R42C3           89

        R43C1           Postage
        R43C3           R5C5*R6C5

        R44C1           Services
        R44C3           2500

        R45C1           Miscellaneous
        R45C3           40

        R46C3           --------

        R47C2           Total
        R47C3           @TOT(R37C3..R45C3)
```

Fig. A-19. Continued from page 163.

Appendix B

Command Summary

The summaries in this appendix are divided into five sections: word processing, file processing, reports, spreadsheets, and communications. These sections are further broken down by menus and keys.

WORD PROCESSING

Use the word processor to create letters, memos, resumes, bills, etc.

THE MAIN MENU

If you want to create a new document, press the 1 key, **Create a document,** from the Main Menu. Press the Esc key to cancel all commands or to leave the menu without selecting a menu item. To add information to the new document, just start typing.

If you want to obtain an existing document, press the 5 key, **Get an existing file,** from the Main Menu. The names of the files that are currently on the disk are listed. The latest file that you worked on is called the Working Copy. It is listed in the directory of your disk under that name. All word processing files have the extension .DOC.

There are two ways of obtaining a file. The first way is to type in the name of the file that you wish to obtain and press the Return or Enter key. The second method is to use the cursor keys to highlight the file and then press the Enter or Return key. If there are more names on the disk that you cannot see, press the PgDn key to see the next list of names. The PgUp key will show you the list of previous names.

If the file you want is on another disk or drive, insert the correct disk and change the directory. For example, insert the disk and type B:Resume or C:\Letter1.

THE F1 HELP KEY

F1 acts as the help key for the Main Menu. If you press F1, First Choice provides a list of basic commands and their uses, as shown in Fig. B-1.

THE F2 SAVE KEY

The document that you are currently working on is the *working copy*. Using the Save Menu accessed from the F2 key, you can choose to save the whole document, save part of the document, merge it with another document, or erase it.

Whole Document. If you want to save the working copy on the disk, press 1, Save a copy of this document, from the Save Menu. You will then be asked to give the document a name. If the document that you wish to save is a revised

Command	Use
F1	Accesses help on the item the cursor is highlighting.
Alt S	Selects text to copies, moved, or erased.
Alt C	Copies selected text to clipboard.
Alt M	Moves selected text to clipboard.
Alt P	Pastes selected text from clipboard.
Alt L	Erases the line the cursor is on.
Alt W	Erases the word the cursor is on.
Alt F	Finds and replaces one word by another.
CTRL Home	Moves the cursor to the beginning of the document.
CTRL End	Moves the cursor to the end of the document.
Home	Moves the cursor to the beginning of the line.
End	Moves the cursor to the end of the line.
PgUp	Moves the cursor to previous screen.
PgDn	Moves the cursor to next screen.

Fig. B-1. The explanations given by the F1 Help key.

version, you may save it under the same name or another name. Saving under the old name overwrites the old version.

Selected Text. If you want to save only a portion of the text, you must first select the text you want to save by moving the cursor to the beginning of the text. Then press the F5 (Edit) key. Move the cursor to the end of the text that you wish to save. Press 2, **Save selected text**, from the Save Menu. Give the selected portion of your text a name, then press the Return or Enter key.

Merge Which File. To combine two files into one, press 3, **Merge which file**, from the Save Menu. Choose or type the name of the file that you wish to merge. The name you type in must be a file that has the extension .DOC or .ASC, or a file that has been printed to disk. Press the Return or Enter key. The document that is merged will be inserted in the document, spreadsheet, file, or report where the cursor is.

Erase Which File. To erase a file, press 4, **Erase which file**. First Choice will present you with a directory or catalog of the disk. Highlight the file that you wish to erase by moving the cursor to it. Press the Return or Enter key. You will be asked if you are sure that you want the file erased. Press the Esc key to keep or save the file. Press the Return or Enter key to erase the file.

THE F3 FEATURES KEY

Pressing the F3 key calls up options to manipulate the words in a document. It is used for such things as finding words, checking spelling, setting margins and tabs, and creating bookmarks.

Find and Replace. If you want to find a word or phrase and replace it by another word or phrase, press 1, **Find and Replace**, from the F3 (Features) menu. If you want to start searching from the beginning of the document, press the CTRL Home keys. If you want to start at some other place in the document, just place your cursor at that point.

You can use the menu to choose the find and replace option, or you can use the ALT F speed key. You will then be asked for the word that you wish to find and the word that you wish to replace it with.

Check Spelling. The Check Spelling option is used to check for typographical errors in documents, form design, or records. To begin the checking of the words, place the cursor where you wish to start. If you want to start the spelling checker at the beginning of the document, press the CTRL Home keys. Press 2, **Check spelling**, from the Features Menu. The spelling checker will look through your document and highlight all words that are not in the master dictionary or your personal dictionary; all words that are repeated; words that are incorrectly capitalized; and all numbers that are not punctuated properly. As First Choice stops at each of the possible erroneous words, you can choose one of the choices that are given, type in the correction of the word, or leave the word alone.

Set Tabs and Indents. All tabs and indents are set from the left margin. Several are already set, but you may set some more. If you want to change a tab or set up a temporary indent, go to the Features Menu. Press 3, **Set tabs and indents.** Position the cursor on the ruler at the bottom of the screen where you want the tab or indent set. If you want to set a tab, type T. If you want to set an indent, type I. Press the Return or Enter key to save the characteristics. Notice that T indicates a tab or > indicates an indent on the ruler at the bottom of the screen. If you want to erase a tab or an indent, just type over it with a Spacebar.

Set Margins and Page Lengths. If you want to change the margins, page length, number the pages, add headers, or add footers, press 4, **Set margins and page length,** from the Features Menu. A menu now appears (Fig. B-2) showing the current settings. If you want to change any of the settings, tab over to that particular setting, type the changes, and press the Return or Enter key to save them. If you change your mind at any time, press the Esc key. You will then be returned to your working copy and no changes will be recorded.

Set Bookmark. Bookmarks are set so that you can move around from place to place. There can be up to six bookmarks and they can be used with documents, records, or spreadsheets. Before you can use bookmarks, all documents, records, or spreadsheets must have been saved. To use a bookmark, move the cursor where you want to set one. Bookmarks cannot be set on a space or another bookmark. From the Features Menu, press 5, **Set bookmark.** The bookmark window will appear. Type in a number from one to six to select the number of the bookmark. When you are finished, press the Return or Enter key. The bookmarks are now set.

Statement	Use
Paper length	Enter the number of lines per page. Default is 66 for 8½ by 11 inch paper.
Left margin	Enter the number of the column that begins the left margin. Default is 10.
Right margin	Enter the number of the column that begins the left margin. Default is 10.
Top and bottom margins	Enter the number of lines for the top and bottom margin. Default is 6.
Header or footer position	Enter C (center), R (right), or L (left) for header or footer position. Default is C (center).
Header or footer style	Enter N (none), U (underline), or B (boldface) for the header or footer style. Default is N (none).
Header or footer line 1, line 2	Enter text for header or footer. You can use only 2 lines for each.

Fig. B-2. The Margin and Page Length Menu, called by choosing 4 from the Features Menu.

Find Bookmark. When you wish to jump to one of your bookmarks, press 6, Find bookmark, from the Features Menu. The bookmark window appears with a listing of all the bookmarks. Highlight the bookmark that you wish to go to and press the Return or Enter key. You will then jump to that particular bookmark.

THE F4 PRINT KEY

The F4 key is used to print an entire document, part of a document, form letters, or labels.

Print This Document. If you want to print the document that you are currently working on, press the F4 key. Then, press 1, Print this document. A list of the print options will be given. Tab over to any item that you wish to change, type in the change, and press the Return or Enter key to register the changes. Printing will then begin.

Print Selected Text Only. You can print out any portion of text that you would like. The text must be located in the working copy. Position the cursor at the beginning of the text that you wish to print. Press the F5 (Edit) key followed by pressing 1, Select text. Move the cursor to the end of the text that you wish to print. Press the F4 (Print) key, then press 2, Print selected text only. A list of the print options will be given. Tab over to any item that you wish to change, type in the change, and press the Return or Enter key to register the changes. Printing will then begin.

Print Form Letters or Labels. Form letters can be printed that combine information from a file into a word processing document, such as a letter. To print a form letter, first type it in the Create a Document Menu. The fields that are to be inserted into the letter must have asterisks (*) around them, as shown below:

Title *First Name* *Last Name*
Address
Town *State* *Zip*

After you finish typing your letter, press the F4 followed by pressing 3, Print form letters or labels. First Choice will ask you for the name of the folder containing the records that you wish to insert in the letter. Type the name of the folder, then press the Return or Enter key. The form letter will be printed.

Print Mailing Labels. To print mailing labels, you must first create a new document that has the fields that you wish to print on the mailing labels. After you have done that, press the F4 key followed by pressing 4, To print mailing labels. Go to the Margins and Page Length Menu and change the paper length to the number of lines from the top of one label to the top of the next. Choose the field names from the file that will appear on the labels. You can search selected records or leave the selection criteria blank and press the F10 key to print mailing labels that contain information in the entire folder.

THE F5 EDIT KEY

The F5 key is used to cut and paste text; erase words, lines, or documents; or select text to be moved, saved, highlighted, etc.

Select Text. You must select text that you wish to copy, move, save, print, or highlight. The command that you choose after selecting text will affect only that text. To select text, place the cursor at the beginning of the block of text that you wish to identify. Press the F5 key, then press 1, **Select text.** You may also use the speed key combination, which is ALT S. Move the cursor to the end of the block that you wish to select.

If you want to change the style of a word or a line, you must select the text before you select an item from the Style Menu.This would include printing text in italics, boldface, underline, etc.

If you change your mind and wish to unselect the text, go back to the Edit Menu or use the speed keys, ALT S. If you return to the Edit Menu, you will notice that the option 1, **Select text**, has become **Unselect text.**

Cut Out Selected Text. The Cut Out option in the Edit Menu erases text from the document. Before you can erase text, you must first select it, using the process just discussed. After you select the text, you can press 2, **Cut out selected text**, from the Edit Menu. The text will be erased. Notice that the space that is created by the erased words is filled in by the surrounding words.

If you accidentally erase text that you would like to have back, don't worry; it is still residing in the clipboard. Position the cursor where you want the text to be inserted. To insert the text back in the document, press 5, **Paste from clipboard**, on the Edit Menu. You may also use the ALT P speed keys. The erased text will be inserted back into the document.

Copy Selected Text to Clipboard. Copying to the clipboard creates a duplicate copy of your text and places it in the clipboard to be used later. If you would like to make a copy of text from the clipboard, press 3, **Copy selected text to clipboard.** You may also use the speed keys, ALT C. Position the cursor where you would like the text inserted. Press 5, **Paste from the clipboard**, or use the ALT P speed keys.

Text can be inserted or pasted into the same document oranother document. When the text is pasted, the words around it are adjusted for the insertion.

Move Selected Text to Clipboard. Moving text is different from copying it. Copying leaves a duplicate of the text in the original location. When you move text, the original text is no longer there. Before you can move text, you must first select it, using the 1 key from the Edit Menu or the ALT S speed keys. Then, press 4, **Move selected text to clipboard.** You can also use the speed keys, ALT M.

Move the cursor to the location at which you wish to have the text and press 5, **Paste from clipboard.** You can also use the speed keys, ALT P. The text will then be inserted at the new location.

Paste From the Clipboard. Any text that is moved to the clipboard may be inserted in a document as many times as you want. You must first select the text that you wish to have moved. The text is then moved or copied to the clipboard by pressing 3, **Copy selected text to clipboard,** or 4, **Move selected text to clipboard.**

Place the cursor at the location where you want to have the text pasted or inserted. Press 5, **Paste from clipboard,** or use the ALT P speed keys. The text is inserted in the document the words around the text are adjusted for spacing.

Insert a Blank Line. There are two ways to insert a blank line in a word processing document. The first way is to move the cursor where you would like to have the line inserted. Then, press 6, **Insert a blank line,** from the Edit Menu. The second method of inserting a blank line is to enter the Insert Mode by pressing the Ins key and then press the Return or Enter key for as many blank lines as you wish to have inserted.

Erase This Word. If you would like to erase the word that the cursor is currently on, press 8, **Erase this word,** from the Edit Menu, or use the ALT W speed keys. The word is erased and the gap created by the deletion is automatically filled in. You can also erase a word by using the Delete key or the Backspace key, which erase words character by character.

Erase This Line. If you would like to erase the line that the cursor is currently on, press 7, **Erase this line,** from the Edit Menu, or use the ALT L speed keys. The line is erased and the following lines, if any, are moved up.

Erase This Document. If you would like to erase the document on which you are currently working (the working copy), press 9,**Erase this document,** from the Edit Menu. Then, press the Return or Enter key. The document will now be erased, enabling you to start another document. If you wish to save the document before you erase the working copy, press the F2 (Save) key, give it a name, and press the Return or Enter key to save it. Now you can delete the working copy.

THE F6 STYLE KEY

The Style Menu enables you to highlight selected text so that you can print it out in boldface, italics, underline, etc. Many of these features depend on the capabilities of your printer. For example, if your printer cannot print italics, highlighting text to be printed in italics will be of no value. Be sure to check the Set Up Equipment option in the Main Menu if you think that your printer should be printing a certain way and it isn't. If you want to leave the Style Menu at any time, press the Esc key.

Boldface. The text that you wish printed in boldface must be selected first. If you do not select the text first, only the first letter or character will be highlighted for boldface. To select the text, press 1, **Select text,** from the Edit Menu. Then press the F6 key followed by pressing the 1 (Boldface) key. The text will be highlighted on the screen.

Underline. The text that you wish printed with an underline must also be selected first, otherwise, only the first letter or character will be highlighted for underline. Press 1, Select text, from the Edit Menu. Then press the F6 key followed by pressing the 2 (Underline) key. The text will be highlighted on the screen.

On some computer screens, the underline will appear as boldface. To find out the style of any characters that are highlighted, place the cursor on the highlight and press the F6 key. All of the different styles will appear in a window (box). A small dot will be next to the styles that those characters possess.

Italics. The text that you wish printed in italics must be selected first. To select the text, press 1, Select text, from the Edit Menu. Then press the F6 key, followed by pressing the 3 (Italics) key. The text will be highlighted on the screen.

Superscript. Text that is highlighted for superscript will be printed slightly higher than the rest of the text. To print text in superscript, first select the text by pressing 1, Select text, from the Edit Menu. Then press the F6 key, followed by pressing the 4 (Superscript) key. The text will be highlighted on the screen.

Subscript. Text that is highlighted for subscript will be printed slightly lower than the rest of the text. To print text in subscript, you must first select it by pressing 1, Select text, from the Edit Menu. Then press the F6 key, followed by pressing the 5 (Subscript) key. The text will be highlighted on the screen.

Erase Style. The Erase Style option changes, or erases, the style that you have chosen. The text that you wish erased must be selected first by pressing 1, Select text, from the Edit Menu. Then press the F6 key, followed by pressing the 6 (Erase Style) key. The text will be highlighted on the screen.

Single Style. An entire document can be single-spaced, or a block of text within a document can be single-spaced. By default, a word processing document is always written using single-spacing. It makes sense to deliberately choose single-spacing only if you are in the double-space mode. To choose single-spacing, select the block of text that you wish to have single-spaced, and press the 7 (Single Space) key from the Features Menu.

Double Space. An entire document can be double-spaced, or a block of text within a document can be double-spaced. If you would like to double-space a complete document, press the 8 (Double Space) key before you start typing in the document. If you wish to double-space only part of a document, select the block of text that you wish to have double-spaced, and press 8, Double Space, from the Features Menu. The block of text that is selected will be double-spaced. Any editing that takes place on the double-spaced block will also be printed using double-spacing.

Even if a document is typed in the single-spaced mode, it can be printed as double-spaced using the double-spaced print option.

Center. Lines and whole blocks of text can be centered. To center a line, place the cursor on that line and press the 9 (Center) key of the Style Menu. The line will automatically be centered.If you want to center a whole block of text, you must first select it by pressing 1, Select text, from the Edit Menu. After you select the text, press the 9 (Center) key of the Style Menu and the text will become centered.

FILE PROCESSING

File processing is used to organize address books, recipe files, customer names, stamp inventories, etc.

CREATING A FILE FOLDER

Before you can enter data into a file, you must design the form so that data can be entered into it at a later time. To create a file folder (or form), press 2 at the Main Menu. You are then asked to give a name to your folder or file. Do not type in the file extension, .FOL, because First Choice will automatically add it to the file name when it saves the file. If you type in the name of a file or folder that is already on the disk, you will be asked if you want to replace the present folder. When you are finished, press the Return or Enter key.

If you want to obtain an existing folder, press 5, Get an existing file, from the Main Menu. The names of the files that are currently on the disk are listed. The latest file that you worked on is called the working copy. It is listed in the directory of your disk under that name.

There are two ways of obtaining a file. The first way is to type in the name of the file that you wish to obtain and press the Return or Enter key. The second method is to use the cursor keys to highlight the file and then press the Enter or Return key. If there are more names on the disk that you cannot see, press the PgDn key to see the next list of names. The PgUp key will show you the list of previous names.

If the file you want is on another disk or drive, insert the correct disk and change the directory. For example, insert the disk and type B:Resume or C:\Letter1.

DESIGNING A FORM

After you have obtained a form, a blank screen will appear where you will type the field names. Field names are items such as first name, last name, address, town, state, telephone number, etc. Field names can be up to 2000 characters long.

To type in a field name, position the cursor on the screen where you would like the field name to appear. Type in the field name followed by a colon (:). After all the field names have been typed in, press the F10 key to save the form design. Once the form is completed, you can enter data into the file or do it later. As you enter data into the folder, notice that the % Full message on the status line changes. The number of records you can save depends on how much memory your computer has and whether you have a floppy or hard disk.

REPORT FEATURE

The report feature of First Choice is used when you want to create a report using the information that was entered in one of the folders or files. A report is created by setting up the print options shown in Fig. B-3 and the formatting commands shown in Fig. B-4, and deciding which fields will appear in the report. To decide the order in which the fields will appear in the report, type a number from 1 to 20 after each field name that you wish to use as a column in the report. The fields will be printed in the order that you number them.

You then give the report a title, deciding on which fields will be sorted. Sorting is performed on columns 1 and 2 in ascending or descending order, depending on what you specify. If you do not want the report to be sorted start numbering the report with column 3. When you are finished numbering the fields, press the F10 key.

You then decide if there are to be any calculations in the report by typing in the calculation options shown in Fig. B-5. There may be several calculations

Statement	Use
Print totals only	If you want to print a summary report which only shows the counts, averages, or totals, type Y.
Pause between pages	If you are using single sheets of paper, type Y. This is useful if you are inserting special stationery or dittos into the printer.
Print to	By default, the output will go to the printer. If you want to look at the report before it is printed, type SCREEN. If you want to have it printed to a disk file to be inserted in a document, type in the name of the disk file. This is also used if you are sending it over communications lines.
Lines per page	Type in the number of lines that are on your sheet of paper. There are normally 66 lines for standard paper that is 8½ by 11 inches. Legal size paper is normally 84 inches long and is 8½ by 14 inches. If you have continuous paper and do not have a page break, type 0. This will bring the type very close to the perforations.
Page width	The default page width is 80. You may type in any number between 1 and 132.
Compressed type	Compressed type is used if you have a very large spreadsheet or report that you wish to reduce so it can fit on 8½ by 11 inch paper. If you type Y, it will print at 17 characters per inch instead of 10 characters per inch which is the default setting. Check your printer manual to see if your printer can print using compressed print.
Draft or correspondence quality	The default is D, which produces a draft copy. Type C to print in letter quality. A lot of printers cannot print in correspondence quality. Check your printer manual.

Fig. B-3. The options available on the Print Options Menu.

Key	Function
•NEW PAGE• or •N•	Causes document to be printed on next page.
•JOIN•	Combines two documents together at printing time.
Page •1•	Each page will be numbered starting with #1.
Page •–1•	First two pages will not be numbered. The third page will be numbered starting with #1.

Fig. B-4. The formatting commands for use with reports.

placed in the same column. For example, SCAT will give the subcount, average and total. **DO NOT** place commas between the letters or you will get an error.

Finally, you decide which records will be printed in the report. The search techniques are shown in Fig. B-6. If you want to include all the records in the report, leave the search instruction form blank. When you are finished, press the F10 key to print the report.

You must always specify the folder or file that you will be using before you create the report. A folder can have numerous reports. A report can have a maximum of 20 columns.

Abbreviation	Meaning	Explanation
T	TOTAL	Adds all the numbers in the column and prints the results.
ST	SUBTOTAL	Gives a subtotal every time the information in column 1 changes. A grand total is printed at the end.
A	AVERAGE	Prints the average at the end of each column.
SA	SUBAVERAGE	Gives a subaverage each time the data in column 1 changes, and an average of all the numbers at the end.
C	COUNT	Counts how many entries are in that column.
SC	SUBCOUNT	Gives a subcount each time the data in column 1 changes and a complete count at the end.
N	NUMERIC	The entry that is typed in is treated numerically. All text is ignored. All decimals are lined up and trailing zeros are added to format the entries.
P	PAGE	When the data in column 1 changes, a new page is started. Only works in column 1.
I	INVISIBLE	A column where the data is used but not printed. Hence, it is invisible.

Fig. B-5. A summary of calculation codes and their meanings.

Search	Meaning	Examples
>$1,000	Finds numbers greater than $1,000	$1,111 $10,987
=$1,000	Finds entry equal to $1,000	$1,000
<$1,000	Finds entry less than $1,000	$999 $454
/ <$1,000	Finds entry greater than $1,000 or equal to $1,000	$2,000
/ . .	Finds any entries that are empty	
/ . . er	Finds any entries that do not end in er	Bob Jane
Jbird	Finds any entry containing Jbird	Jbird
. .	Finds fields that have entries	Bruno
. . zy	Finds any entry ending in zy	Waszy
Was . .	Finds any entry beginning with Was	Waszy
. . uk . .	Finds any entry that contains a uk	fluke
87/ . . / . .	Any entry that contains 1987	87/12/30 87/01/02
?aid	Finds a four letter entry ending in aid	said maid
dat?	Finds four letter entry beginning with dat	date data
w??e	Finds a four-letter entry beginning with w and ending with e	wire were

Fig. B-6. A summary of search techniques.

SPREADSHEETS

Spreadsheets present data as cells in a table. A change in the data in one cell is instantly reflected by changes in any related cells. Spreadsheets are typically used for accounting and other financial applications because they aid decision-making.

CREATE A SPREADSHEET

If you want to start a new spreadsheet, press 4, Create a spreadsheet, from the Main Menu. If you want to obtain an existing spreadsheet, press 5, Get an existing file, from the Main Menu. The names of the files that are currently on the disk are listed. The latest file that you worked on is called the working copy. It is listed in the directory of your disk under that name.

There are two ways of obtaining a file. The first way is to type in the name of the file that you want to obtain and then press the Return or Enter key. The second method is to use the cursor keys (Fig. B-7) to highlight the file and then press the Enter or Return key. If there are more names on the disk that you cannot see, press the PgDn key to see the next list of names. The PgUp key will show you the list of previous names.

If the file you want is on another disk or drive, insert the correct disk and change the directory. For example, insert a disk and type B:Resume or C:>Letter1.

Cursor Keys	Movement
ALT Q	Start/stop quick entry
ALT R	Recalculate spreadsheet
ALT F	Edit or type cell formula
ALT G	Go to a cell
ALT W	Erase this cell
ALT S	Select cell or cells
ALT C	Copy selected cells to clipboard
ALT M	Move selected cells to clipboard
ALT P	Paste from clipboard
ALT T	Set cell type
CTRL HOME	Go to cell R1C1
CTRL END	Go to last cell of spreadsheet
HOME	Go to beginning of current row
END	Go to end of current row
TAB	Go to next cell in row
SHIFT TAB	Go to previous cell in row
ENTER or RETURN	Go to next cell in column
CTRL ENTER or CTRL RETURN	Go to previous cell in column
PgUp	Go to next screen
PgDn	Go to previous screen
CTRL PgUp	Move sideways left one screen
CTRL PgDn	Move sideways right one screen

Fig. B-7. The cursor keys used with spreadsheets.

THE F2 SAVE KEY

If you want to save the spreadsheet or any part of it, press the F2 (Save) key. This saves a copy of the spreadsheet that is in the working copy and saves it to the disk under another name. After you press the F2 (Save) key, you will be prompted for a name. Type in a name followed by pressing the Enter or Return key. The extension .SS is automatically added to the spreadsheet name. If you want to save the spreadsheet as an ASCII file, type in the name followed by the extension .ASC. This is used if you would like to send the file over the telephone to another computer.

Another option that is used with the F2 key, is to erase a file. You can choose **Erase a file** from the Save menu when you are within the spreadsheet application. First Choice will give you a list of the files that are on the disk. Select the file that you wish to erase by using the cursor keys or typing in the name of the file. After you press the Return or Enter key the file will automatically be erased from the disk.

THE F3 FEATURES KEY

The F3 key is used to recalculate automatically or manually, edit a formula, go to a cell, start quick entry, or set and find bookmarks.

Recalculate. This menu item is only used if you have set the calculation to manual. If you have made several changes to the spreadsheet using the manual calculation, you will have to recalculate every time you wish the changes to be effective. ALT R is the speed key combination that will enable you to use the recalculation mode.

If you leave the spreadsheet in the automatic recalculation mode, there is no reason to recalculate. Every time you leave a cell the spreadsheet will automatically be recalculated.

Type or Edit Cell Formula. When you press 2, **Type or edit cell formula**, from the Features Menu, the formula box will appear in the window in the bottom right of the screen. This item is chosen if you wish to give the cell a name, give a value to a cell, or place a formula into the cell. Formulas are created the IF-THEN-ELSE operators shown in Fig. B-8 and the keywords and financial functions shown in Fig. B-9. ALT F is the speed key combination that will give you the formula box.

Set Manual Recalculation. By default, First Choice will recalculate each cell after a change is made and you leave that particular cell. This can be very time-consuming, especially if you have an extremely large spreadsheet. You can set the spreadsheet to manual recalculation by pressing 3, **Set manual recalculation**. Recalculations are not performed until you tell the program that you wish to do so. When you are ready to recalculate the spreadsheet, simply press the ALT R speed keys.

BE CAREFUL! It is very easy to forget that you must recalculate the spreadsheet. When you are learning how to use the spreadsheet, always stay

Operator	Meaning	Example
=	equal to	If Sales = 3,000 then Tax = 0.05
<	less than	If Sales < 3,000 then Tax = 0.04
>	greater than	If Sales > 3,000 then Tax = 0.06
> =	greater than or equal to	If Sales > = 3,000 then Tax = 0.06
< =	less than or equal to	If Sales < = 3,000 then Tax = 0.05
< >	not equal to	If Sales < > 0 then Tax = 0.03
AND	two conditions must be true	If (Sales > $3,000) AND (Bonus > $50) then Tax = 0.05
OR	one condition must be true	If (Sales > $3,000) OR (Bonus > $50) then Tax = 0.03
NOT	negates condition	If NOT (Sales > $3,000) then Tax = 0.05 else Tax = 0.03 MEANING: If sales is greater than $3,000 then tax is 0.03. If sales is less than or equal to $3,000, the tax is 0.05.

(NOTE: Parentheses are not required but are very useful in understanding the statements.)

Fig. B-8. The operators used with IF-THEN-ELSE statements.

in the automatic recalculation mode. To go back to the recalculation mode, press the **Set automatic recalculation** key from the Features Menu.

Go To a Cell. For quick movement throughout a spreadsheet, you can go to any cell coordinate, cell name, specific row, or specific column. This can be accomplished by pressing 4, **Go to a cell**, key from the Features Menu and specifying the cell name or coordinate. The ALT G is the speed key combination to go to any particular cell.

Start Quick Entry. The quick entry feature is used to quickly add row headings, column headings, or formulas to any cell or group of cells that you wish. If you want to change headings, type the first heading or use the heading that is already there. Press the Tab key if you want to add column headings or press the Enter or Return key if you wish to do row headings. ALT Q is the speed key combination to start the quick entry. Some examples of quick entry headings are shown in Fig. B-10.

If you wish to use the speed keys for formulas, position the cursor where you want to start entering the formulas. Press the ALT F key combination to type in or edit the formula. Use the existing formula or type in a new formula. Press the ALT Q speed key combination and use the cursor movement keys to advance to the next cell. The formula will automatically be placed in that cell. If any cell references have to be changed in that cell, they will be automatically done.

Command	Explanation
ABS(X)	Computes the absolute value of X.
ACOS(X)	Computes the angle whose cosine equals X in radians, where X is between −1 and 1.
ASIN(X)	Computes the angle whose sine equals X in radians, where X is between −1 and 1.
ATAN(X)	Computes the angle in radians whose tangent equals X.
AVG(X)	Computes the average of all values in the range.
COS(X)	Computes the cosine of X, where X is an angle in radians.
COUNT(X)	Counts the number of cells that have numeric data in them.

FV ON(amount)
AT(rate)
OVER(periods)

Computes the future value of a series of equal payments at a certain rate over a period of time. For example, consider:

FV ON(100) AT(10%/12) OVER(3*12) = $4,178.18.

You are dividing and multiplying by 12 to give you the monthly interest rate.

IF(condition)
THEN(value)
ELSE(value)

Gives different values, depending on the outcome of the conditions
For example, consider this statement:

IF SALES > 1000 Then TAX = .1 Else TAX = .05

This means if the values of sales is over $1000, the tax is 10% otherwise the tax is 5%.

INTEREST ON(amount)
AT(rate)
OVER(# of periods)
FOR(period)

Calculates the amount of interest you will have paid in a series of payments at a given interest rate on a loan. For example, consider this statement:

INTEREST ON(50000) AT(.115/12) OVER(15*12) FOR(12) = $149.51

Gives the amount of interest during the twelfth monthly payment on a $50,000 15 year loan at an interest rate of 11.5%.

LOOKUP(value)
IN(range)
ACROSS(columns)

Looks up a value in a range of cells and places the result in a cell.

	C1	C2	C3
R12	Sales	Rate	Bonus
R13	0	0.05	0
R14	1000	0.06	20
R15	3000	0.07	40
R16	5000	0.08	60

Fig. B-9. The keywords and financial functions used to create spreadsheet formulas.

Command	Explanation
	If you type in the keyword expression LOOKUP 4567 IN (R13C1 . . R16C1) ACROSS 2, the value of 40 will be placed in the cell. The number 4567 is between R15C1 and R16C1. It rounds down to 3000 and goes two across to find the Bonus value of 40.
MAX(range) or MAXIMUM(range)	Finds the largest value in a range of cells.
MIN(range) or MINIMUM(range)	Finds the smallest value in a range of cells.
NPV AT(interest rate) OF(range)	Finds the net present value of a series of future cash flows. The interest rate is the cost of money that is used to discount the future cash flows or the discount rate. The range is a series of cells found in one column or row that contain the amount of cash payments after the initial cash outlay. For example, NPV AT(10%/12) OF(R5C4 . . R5C7) gives the current cash value of the payments in Row 5, Columns 4 through 7, when discounted at a 10% annual rate.
PAYMENT ON(amount) AT(interest rate) OVER(# of periods)	Computes the payment you need to make on a loan over a given time period at a specific interest rate. For example, PAYMENT ON($50,000) AT(.115/12) OVER(15*12) = $584.09 computes the mortgage payment on a $50,000 loan at 11.5% annual interest for a period of 15 years which is $584.09.
PV ON(amount) AT(rate) OVER(# of periods)	Computes the present value of a series of equal payments at a specific interest rate over a specified period of time. For example, PV ON($100) AT(10%) OVER 3 = $248.69 gives you the present value of a series of three $100 payments at 10% interest is $248.69.
ROUND(X) TO (Y)	Rounds the value of X to Y decimal places. If you want to round off to the nearest integer, set Y to 0 or leave off the number following the TO.
SIN(X)	Computes the sine of X, where X is measured in radians.
STDEV(range) or STD(range)	Computes the standard deviation of the values in the range.
TAN(X)	Computes the tangent of X, where X is measured in radians.
TOTAL(range) or TOT(X)	Calculates the sum of the values in the range.
VAR(range) VARIANCE(range)	Computes the variance of all values in the range.

Entry	Quick Entry Gives
Mon	Tues, Weds, . . .
Monday	Tuesday, Wednesday, . . .
March	April, May, . . .
Apr	May, Jun, . . .
Qtr 1	Qtr 2, Qtr 3, . . .
Year 87	Year 88, Year 89, . . .
Week 10	Week 11, Week 12, . . .
Dec 87	Jan 88, Feb 88, . . .

Fig. B-10. Some headings produced by the quick entry keys.

Set Bookmark. Bookmarks are set so that you can move around from place to place. There can be up to six bookmarks, and they can be used with documents, records, or spreadsheets. Before you can use bookmarks, all documents, records, or spreadsheets must have been saved.

To use a bookmark, move the cursor where you want to set one. Bookmarks cannot be set on a space or another bookmark. From the Features menu, press 5, Set bookmark. The bookmark window will now appear. Type in a number from one to six to select the number of the bookmark. When you are finished, press the Return or Enter key. The bookmarks are set.

Find Bookmark. When you wish to jump to one of your bookmarks, press 6, Find bookmark, from the Features Menu. The bookmark window will appear with a listing of all the bookmarks. Highlight the bookmark that you wish to find and press the Return or Enter key. You will then jump to that particular bookmark.

THE F4 PRINT KEY

Using the F4 key, you can print an entire spreadsheet or just print selected cells from a spreadsheet.

Print This Spreadsheet. If you want to print the spreadsheet that you are currently working on, press the F4 key. Then select 1, Print this document. A list of the print options will be given. Tab over to any item that you wish to change, type in the change, and press the Return or Enter key to register the changes. Printing will then begin.

Print Selected Cells Only. You can print out any portion of the spreadsheet that you would like. The spreadsheet must be located in the working copy. Position the cursor in the upper-leftmost cell that you wish to start printing. Press the F5 (Edit) key followed by pressing 1, Select cells. Move the cursor to the lower-rightmost cell at which you wish the printing to end. Press the F4 key followed by pressing 2,**Print selected cells only**. A list of the print options will be given. Tab over to any item that you wish to change, type in the new change, and press the Return or Enter key to register the changes. Printing will begin.

THE F5 EDIT KEY

The F5 key is used to erase, copy, move and paste selected cells; to insert or cut out rows or columns; or to erase the cell or spreadsheet currently in use.

Select Cells. You must select cells that you wish to copy, move, save, or print later. The commands will affect only the selected text. To select cells, place the cursor at the upper-leftmost cell of the block of cells you wish to identify. Press the F5 key followed by pressing 1, **Select cells**. You may also use the speed keys, ALT S. Move the cursor to the lower-rightmost cell of the block you wish to identify by using the cursor keys.

You must select cells if you wish to save only selected cells, print only selected cells, move or copy cells, copy or cut out selected cells to the clipboard.

If you change your mind and wish to unselect the cell, go back to the Edit Menu or use the speed keys, ALT S. If you return to the Edit Menu, notice that option 1, **Select cells**, has become **Unselect cells**.

Erase Selected Cells. The option to erase selected cells erases the contents and formulas of cells from the spreadsheet. Before you can erase cells, you must first select the cells. Press the F5 key followed by pressing 1, **Select cells**. You may also use the speed keys, ALT S. Move the cursor to the lower-rightmost cell of the block you wish to identify by using the cursor keys. After you select the cells, you can press 2, **Erase selected cells**, from the Edit Menu. The cells will be erased. Notice that the space that is created by the erased cells is filled in by the surrounding cells.

If you accidentally erase cells that you would like back, don't worry; they are still residing in the clipboard. Position the cursor where you want the cells to be inserted. To return or insert the cells back in the document, press 5, **Paste from clipboard**, in the Edit Menu. You may also use the ALT P speed keys. The erased cells will be inserted back into the document.

Copy Selected Cells to Clipboard. Copying cells to the clipboard creates a duplicate copy of your cells in the clipboard to be used at a later time. If you would like to make a copy of cells from the clipboard, press 3, **Copy selected cells to clipboard**. You may also use the speed keys, ALT C. Position the cursor where you would like the cells inserted. Press 5, **Paste from the clipboard**, or use the ALT P speed keys.

Cells can be inserted or pasted into one spreadsheet or another document. When a cell is pasted, the cells around it are adjusted for the insertion.

Move Selected Cells to Clipboard. Moving is different from copying in that copying leaves a duplicate of the cells in the original location. When you move cells, the original cells are no longer there.

Before you can move cells, you must first select them. Place the cursor at the beginning of the cells that you wish moved and press 1, **Select cells**, from the Edit Menu, or use the ALT S speed keys. Finish moving the cursor to the end of the cells that you wish moved. Then, press 4, **Move selected cells to clipboard**, from the Edit Menu. You can also use the speed keys ALT M.

Move the cursor to the location at which you wish to have the cells placed and press 5, **Paste from clipboard**. You can also use the speed keys, ALT P. The cells will be inserted at the new location.

Paste From the Clipboard. Any cells that are moved to the clipboard may be inserted in the document as many times as you want. You must first select the cells that you wish to have moved by pressing 1, **Select cells**, from the Edit Menu. The cells are moved or copied to the clipboard by pressing 3, **Copy selected cells to clipboard**, or 4, **Move selected cells to clipboard**.

Place the cursor at the location that you wish to have the cells pasted or inserted. Press the 5 **Paste from clipboard key** or use the ALT P speed keys. The cells are inserted in the spreadsheet and the cells around them are adjusted for spacing.

Insert Row/Column. To insert a row or column, move the cursor where you would like to have the line inserted. Press 6, **Insert row/column** from the Edit Menu.

Cut Out Row/Column. If you would like to erase a row or column that the cursor is currently on, press 7, **Cut out row/column**, in the Edit Menu. This operation erases the cell the cursor is on and closes any gaps. If you would like to erase just the contents or formulas of a cell, choose **Erase This Cell**, which is discussed next.

Erase This Cell. If you would like to erase the name, value, and formula of a cell that the cursor is currently on, press 8, **Erase this cell**, in the Edit Menu or use the ALT W speed keys. The cell is erased and the gap created by the deletion is automatically filled in.

Erase This Spreadsheet. If you would like to erase the spreadsheet that you are currently working on (the working copy), press 9, **Erase this document**, from the Edit menu followed by pressing the Return or Enter key. The document will be erased, enabling you to start another document. All the contents and formulas of the cells will be erased.

If you wish to save the spreadsheet before you erase the working copy, press the F2 (Save) key, give the spreadsheet a name, and press the Return or Enter key to save it. Now you can delete the working copy.

THE F6 STYLE KEY

The F6 key is used to change the style of individual cells in a spreadsheet, or to change the style of all of the cells in a spreadsheet.

Set Cell Style. Set Cell Style changes the style of an individual cell by overriding the global cell style. It is used to insert dollar signs, commas, etc.,

Currency Symbol	Meaning
$	Dollar
£	Pound
F	Franc (general)
FF	French franc
BF	Belgian franc
SFr	Swiss franc
DM	Germa mark
L	Lire (general)
Lit	Italian lire
Kr	Swedish krone
P	Peso (general)
Pts	Spanish peseta
S	Schilling (general)
öS	Austrian schilling
R	Rand or ruble
Y	Japanese yen

Fig. B-11. Currency symbols that can be used with the Set Global Style option.

in a particular cell. It may be used for an individual cell or a group of cells. To change the style of a particular cell, place the cursor on that cell and press 1, **Set cell style**, of the Style Menu or press the ALT T speed key combination. If you are changing the style of a group of cells, you must first press 1, **Select cells**, from the Edit Menu and then press 1, **Set cell style**, from the Style Menu.

Set Global Style. The global style is set to show how the entire spreadsheet will be displayed. By default, First Choice starts with commas and two decimal places. If you want to change any or all of them, tab over to the entry that you wish to change and make the desired changes. First Choice can use up to 14 numeric digits or 20 characters for each value in a cell, including the currency symbols shown in Fig. B-11.

To generate the £ on your keyboard, press the ALT key while typing the numbers 156 on the numeric keypad (it will not work if you type the numbers

Key	Function
CTRL S	Enables you to stop transmission.
CTRL Q	Lets you start transmission.
ESC	Return to First Choice Main Menu. Depends on service that is being used.
CTRL Backspace	Enables you to backspace if you make an error.

Fig. B-12. The keys used for communication.

	Communication Services
CompuServe	General interest information utility. Call 1-800-848-8199 for more information.
Dialog Business Connection	Provides business information on different industries. Call 1-800-3-DIALOG for more information.
Dow Jones/Retrieval	Provides access to latest stock quotes, financial news, and Wall Street Journal Highlights. Call 1-800-257-5114 for more information.
MCI Mail	Provides service to computer postal system. Call 1-800-MCI-2255 for more information.
OAG	Official Airline Guide provides information on flights. Call 1-800-323-3537 for more information.
The Source	Provides general information on many topics. Call 1-800-336-3300 for more information.
Answer Incoming Call	Tells your computer to prepare for a call from another computer that is equipped with similar communications software.
Other Service	You can type in any service that is not listed. Its name can have a maximum of 20 characters.

Fig. B-13. Some communications services that First Choice supports.

at the top of the keyboard). To generate the ö on your keyboard, press the ALT key while typing the numbers 148 on the numeric keypad. When you are finished typing in the three numbers, release the ALT key.

COMMUNICATION

Your computer can communicate with others by sending signals through a modem over telephone lines. The keys that are used by First Choice for communication are shown in Fig. B-12. The communications services that First Choice supports are shown in Fig. B-13.

Glossary

Glossary

access time—The elapsed interval between entry of an instruction and completion of its execution. Typically, this term refers to entry from a terminal and display of requested data for the user.

acoustic coupler—A modem in which the handset of a telephone is placed.

ASCII—A coding system used to represent all text characters and control codes a computer is capable of producing. An acronym for American Standard Code for Information Interchange.

back-up copy—A copy of any file or disk that you create (and store someplace else) to protect against possible disasters to the original file.

baud rate—A way of measuring data transmission speeds. It is usually measured in bits per second.

bit (binary digit)—A single character in a binary number system, i.e., a binary one or a binary zero.

block—A group of words in the word processing module to be moved, copied, or deleted.

boldfacing—Printing characters so that they are darker than ordinary printed characters.

byte—A group of adjacent bits operated on as a unit by a digital computer.

cell—A spreadsheet location at the intersection of a row and a column where data can be entered.

centering—Moving text on a line so that there are an equal number of blank spaces on either side of the text.

character—A letter, number, space, punctuation mark, or any other symbol that can be typed from the computer's keyboard.

column—A vertical position on the screen. The screen accommodates up to 80 characters or spaces across each line. Each position is called a column.

column break—The place in a sorted report where a value changes.

common carrier—A company that specializes in offering standard telephone lines that are leased for data communications.

cos—A library function that finds the cosine of a number.

CTRL—A key on most personal computers that is used in conjunction with other keys to execute certain commands.

cursor—The pointer on the screen that indicates to the user where the next entry is to be made.

data—Coded information. Any representations such as characters or analog quantities to which real-world meaning is assigned.

data communications—The technology that enables electronic transmission of data from one location to another.

date field—All dates that need to be accessed or sorted must be typed in the form YY/MM/DD.

derived column—In the report section, a column created from calculations performed on other columns (rather than from information directly available from an existing field on a form).

dial-up service—An information service that is accessed over telephone lines.

direct-connect modem—A type of modem that is wired directly into a telephone instrument.

directory—A list of names of files stored on a disk.

document—A piece of writing produced with a word processor.

download—To send programs or files from a mainframe to a personal computer.

downtime—Any interval during which a computer system is inoperative because of a malfunction.

electronic mail—A computer-based system in which conventional mail messages are transmitted from their sources to their destinations by electronic means.

electronic spreadsheet—A software package that stores data in rows and columns. The user can manipulate these data by issuing commands.

electronic telecommuting—A computer-based system that allows employees to work in their homes or in a local office. They communicate their accomplishments from computer terminal to computer terminal via high-volume communications channels.

field—The smallest unit of information in a data file. Each field contains only one piece of information, such as a name, age, and so on.

file—A collection of related records stored on a disk and given a name.

file folder—A collection of records that contain the same type of information.

file name—A name given to a file. A file name can contain up to eight characters.

financial statement—A set of documents that summarizes financial condition. A set of financial statements includes an income statement, a balance sheet, and a statement of changes in financial condition.

form—A way of organizing related information about people, places, ideas, etc.

form letter—A type of business letter that contains a standard body of text and is mailed to multiple parties.

format—A general plan of arrangement, organization, or style. To place into a form or style. The physical arrangement of text on documents or data on storage media.

formatting commands—A type of instruction within the print routine of a word processing package that specifies how text will be printed on a page or form.

formula—A specific calculation or system of calculations that defines the quantitative relationships between numbers appearing on a spreadsheet.

full duplex—A type of communication channel that is set up to send and receive signals simultaneously in both directions.

function—Special formulas predefined by the spreadsheet software to perform certain mathematical operations, such as summing and finding an average.

function keys—Keys that are labelled F1 through F6 that are used to perform specific tasks such as saving and printing documents.

future value—The value of an initial investment after a specified period of time at a certain rate of interest.

half duplex—A type of communication channel that can send and receive signals in one direction at a time.

handshaking—A descriptive term for establishing a data transmission protocol that is acceptable to both sending and receiving devices.

hard copy—A paper document or computer output.

header—A notation at the top of each page of a document.

help commands—Keyboard entries that are available that display user assistance by pressing the F1 function key.

highlighting—Enhanced or reversed coloration of a cell or option. Highlighting usually indicates that the cursor or pointer is in that position.

information service—A dial-up service linking individual users with computer systems that store statistics and textual information for reference.

integrated software—Software containing word processing, database management, electronic spreadsheets and other functions and the capability to blend these functions easily.

invisible column—In the report section, a column used for calculation and reference purposes that isn't displayed or printed in a final report.

join—A command that merges two documents together at printing time. The two files that are joined are not added together to the working copy.

justify—To make typed information in a document line up at the left margin (left justify), right margin (right justify), or line up with both the left and right margins.

K—Equivalent to approximately 1000 bytes of storage. In actuality, it is 1024 bytes.

label—A word, phrase, or value used to identify a document, file, or program.

log—A library function that finds the logarithm of a number.

lookup table—A table of values used to fill out information blanks automatically.

mail merge—A capability of the word processor that allows the user to merge data from different files and to perform special printing tasks.

main menu—A list of the processing options offered by a program, usually displayed at the start of an application session.

margins—The setting that determines the leftmost and rightmost boundaries of a text line.

margin bottom—The number of blank lines that will be preserved between the last line of text and the bottom edge of the page.

margin top—The number of blank lines that will be preserved between the top edge of the paper and the first line of text.

menu—A screen display indicating the choices that you have. A user can select the desired option from the menu.

merge document—A document you type once but use many times by adding special merge fields. The merge fields take information from your database and combine the information with your document. The end result is a series of documents with personalized information.

merge file—Any First Choice file used with a merged document.

modem—A device that converts digital data signals so that they can be transmitted over communication lines. It is an abbreviation for modulator-demodulator.

mouse—A specific type of computer input device. The user slides the mouse along a horizontal surface and depresses one or more buttons located on its top to rearrange the material on the display screen to control various computer operations.

net present value (NPV)—The present value of a project's future cash flow less the initial investment in the project.

new page—A command inserted in a document, resulting in a page break. It moves the information to the top of the next sheet of paper and continues to print.

page break—The point in a document or report where a new page is to start.

parallel printer—A type of printer which receives transmission of data as a group of bits or signals. A parallel printer is much faster than a serial printer, which receives data one bit at a time.

parity checking—An automatic error-detection procedure that uses extra checking bits that are carried along with the numerical bits being processed.

personal dictionary—Words added to your own personal dictionary as abbreviations, special words used at work, and names of people and companies. It is saved under the name PERSONAL.FC.

port—The point of interface between the computer and other peripherals, such as a printer. Ports are either serial or parallel.

precedence—The order in which the parts of a formula are calculated.

present value—The cash value, today, of future returns.

print options—The screen settings that tell you line spacing, number of copies, and the destination (parallel or serial printer, modem, disk) of the printed file.

printer control code—The decimal ASCII equivalent of a particular printer's control codes. It makes the printer add special effects to a printed report or document.

protocol—An established set of rules for transmitting and receiving data.

record—A form that is filled in with information. It is a set of information about one object, person, unit, etc. Each record is made up of separate fields of data.

rounded—Data that has been adjusted so that it more accurately represents a specific value in the number of positions desired. For example, 19.979 rounded to two decimal places is 19.98.

row—A horizontal line of data values within a data table or spreadsheet.

ruler line—A line of information on the screen. The ruler line shows the maximum possible length of the text line and the position of tabs.

scroll—Moving the cursor so that different parts of the text, file, or spreadsheet are on the screen.

serial printer—A type of printer that receives transmission from the CPU one signal at a time.

sin—A library function that finds the sine of an angle.

sorting—All reports in First Choice are sorted using column 1. It can be in ascending or descending order.

spelling checker—This utility proofreads your document for typing and spelling mistakes, repeated words, words that are incorrectly capitalized, and numbers that are punctuated incorrectly.

spreadsheet—A document that presents data in a table format to assist in making comparisons.

sqr—A library function that finds the square root of a number.

start bit—A bit added to a byte to signal its beginning for transmission purposes.

status line—A line of information on the screen. The status line indicates the position of the cursor on the page of text.

stop bits—One or more bits added to a byte to signal its end for transmission purposes.

submenu—A secondary menu providing further definitions or processing options beyond those contained in a main menu.

subscriber service—An on-line facility that enables a user, for a fee, to access a wide variety of programs and data bases. Many subscriber services provide access to the Dow Jones Industrial Averages, news services, hotel and airplane reservation networks, etc.

summary report—A report that shows only totals and subtotals.

summing—Adding up the contents of a specified field for all records that meet a specified condition.

tabs—Preset positions to which the user can move the cursor by pressing the Tab key. Tab positions can be set or removed as needed.

tan—A library function that finds the tangent of a number.

telecommuting—An arrangement under which people work at home on computers, receiving assignments from and delivering work to a computer at the organization's offices.

teleprocessing—A reference to techniques under which data are represented to a computer from remote locations through the use of telephone lines.

transfer rate—The speed at which data are transmitted between computers and peripheral devices. Measured in bits per second, or baud.

up time—A period of time during which a computer or computer system is operable and accessible for processing.

upload—The process of sending files from a personal computer to a mainframe.

wildcard— A character that stands for any character or group of characters. The wildcard for any individual character is the question mark (?). The wildcard for any group of characters is two consecutive dots (..).

word processing—The computer-aided preparation of documents. It involves manipulating words and characters by entering and storing them in a computer, for the purpose of efficiently producing written documents.

word wrap—A text editing feature that automatically moves a word to the next line if it cannot fit on the previous one.

working copy—The word processing document, record, or spreadsheet that you are presently working on. It can be saved any time by giving it a name.

worksheet—Another term for an electronic worksheet.

Index

195

Edited by Marianne Krcma

Other Bestsellers From TAB

Other Bestsellers From TAB